THE COFFEE SELF-TALK DAILY READER #1

BITE-SIZED NUGGETS OF MAGIC TO ADD TO
YOUR MORNING ROUTINE

KRISTEN HELMSTETTER

*Green
Butterfly
Press*

Coffee Self-Talk Daily Reader #1

Copyright © 2021 by Kristen Helmstetter

ISBN: 978-1-7362735-6-2

For information on excerpting, reprinting or licensing portions of this book, please write to info@greenbutterflypress.com.

v1.0

ABOUT THE AUTHOR

In 2018, Kristen Helmstetter sold everything to travel the world with her husband and daughter. She currently lives in a medieval hilltop town in Umbria, Italy.

She writes romance novels under the pen name Brisa Starr.

Kristen is "designing her life with intention," and she invites you to join her on the journey at:

HappySexyMillionaire.me

And on Instagram:

 instagram.com/coffeeselftalk

CONTENTS

PREFACE

Why a Daily Reader?

One year ago, I wrote the book, *Coffee Self-Talk*. Since its release, the book has gained a large following and a thriving, nurturing community of readers in its Facebook group at facebook.com/groups/coffeeselftalk. It has been wonderful to see all of the love, support, and laughs that the members provide to each other every day of the week.

In the comments there and elsewhere in social media, two themes caught my attention:

First, some people had expected *Coffee Self-Talk* to be a daily reader, presumably from the book's subtitle, *5 minutes a day to start living your magical life*. Some readers thought this meant, "read this book for five minutes a day." But *Coffee Self-Talk* was not structured as a daily reader. Rather, it's a regular book that outlines a process for developing your own five-minute (or more) daily self-talk program.

Second, when people finished reading the book, many of them simply wanted more. In fact, a lot of people have reported that they immediately started reading the book a second time.

For these reasons, and because I had a lot more to say, I decided to give my readers what they were asking for: A daily reader, based on the ideas presented in *Coffee Self-Talk*. Daily, bite-sized nuggets to get you thinking more about what matters each day, and taking action on creating your magical life.

And here it is!

This book will deepen your connection to yourself, to others, and to the flow of the new, epic life you're building. The aim of this book is to give you a little tidbit each day of something to think about, or do, that'll make you happier and help you manifest your dream life faster.

My reason for writing *The Coffee Self-Talk Daily Readers* (that's plural, as this is the first in a series) is to help you while you're in the middle of making life changes using Coffee Self-Talk. Think of this as a booster shot. Daily pick-me-ups of happiness and love, ways to add feel-good feelings as you surf the waves of life, and tips for ensuring your success.

This book is not meant to replace your daily Coffee Self-Talk routine that you do with your script. No. This book is for the five-minutes *after* your Coffee Self-Talk time. It's for the people who are pumped up, on fire, changing their lives, and wanting to set themselves up for epically successful wins in every way.

Note: If you haven't read *Coffee Self-Talk* yet, I recommend that you read it. While it's not required reading for this Daily Reader, the material it covers is the foundation for your life change. This Daily Reader will still be useful, with all its tips for helping you live a happier and more effective life, but *Coffee Self-Talk* is like the cake, and this Daily Reader is the icing on that cake.

If you are new to Coffee Self-Talk (or if you'd like a quick review), I have included a two-page Coffee Self-Talk primer right after the Introduction. Please feel free to skip it if you have recently read *Coffee Self-Talk.*

INTRODUCTION

Dear friend,

The daily routine outlined in the book, *Coffee Self-Talk*, is changing tens of thousands of people's lives. And if you haven't started doing the routine yet, it can change your life, in both the short term and the long term.

In the short term, during those moments when you're actually reading your Coffee Self-Talk scripts in the morning (or listening to recorded scripts), life feels good, you feel amazing, and love pours out of you. (Or it will soon, if you keep it up!) You feel the effects as you're doing it. In the present.

And most days, your Coffee Self-Talk routine will infuse your entire day with powerful, dream-manifesting juice. These are more short-term benefits, lasting throughout the day. Over time however, the things you say and feel during your morning ritual become ingrained in the grooves of your brain, the beats of your heart, and the sparkles in your soul. You start to rewire your brain to become the person you want to be, and to live the life you want to live. This becomes the default you, over time—a new you, living a new life. These are the long-term benefits.

So, the long-term advantage is that you're changing your *you.* Your personality. The way you command the ship of your life. You're also drawing your dreams and goals and manifestations to you. (The process by which all this happens is explained in detail in *Coffee Self-Talk.*)

But, in the beginning of your epic transformation, you might sometimes have gaps between the times you do your morning Coffee Self-Talk ritual—the space from one morning to the next—where you could benefit from a little extra boost of love, peace, energy, or simply reminding. The activities in this book are like an afternoon shot of espresso—like they do in Italy—to get you through the rest of the day.

You may have heard a similar idea about mindfulness meditation. People say it's good to meditate once a day, right? You'll reap short and long-term benefits from this daily practice. But if you get off the couch from your meditation, and you return to your usual habits—the old you —then it will take much longer to start seeing those long-term benefits you desire. The real power from meditation comes when you operate mindfully, even when you're *not* meditating. When you become mindfully self-aware *at all times.*

It's the same idea with Coffee Self-Talk, and the elevated

state that you get into while doing the ritual. You want to find ways to keep the juju going when you're not sipping your morning cup of coffee.

On your path to self-manifesting badassery, you want to do everything possible to set yourself up for success, and that includes all those hours during the day when you're away from the kitchen table, breakfast nook, patio, comfy couch, or cozy bed where you do your Coffee Self-Talk. You want cool tools and clever tricks up your sleeve, ready at a moment's notice, while surfing the waves of daily life, and building the new you with your Coffee Self-Talk.

But sometimes you get caught up in to-do's of life, or your circumstances change, and your elevated energy dips. Or even nosedives. This book is to help keep you on track during such times. It's filled with easy tips and activities to help you keep the infusion of awesomeness going all day long. The fun activities here will equip you with tools to thrive through the dips and bumps, allowing you to maintain your high feelings most of the time. It takes a bit of work, but it's fun stuff. It's all about maintaining the proper mindset and creating habits that will ensure your success.

Immersion: The Key to Manifesting More Quickly

You've probably heard that the best way to learn a foreign language is with "immersion," which means surrounding yourself with the new language, all day, every day. Such as moving to a country where that language is spoken, or going to a school where they only speak that language, even outside of class.

It's no wonder then, that language immersion students learn fast! Why? Because they're focused on it 100%. They have no choice but to learn it!

That's how I'm currently learning Italian. By living in Italy, I've picked up the language faster because it's everywhere I turn... walking into town, at the grocery store, the cafe, or on the bus, the TV, conversations with the neighbors, and so on. I'm totally immersed in it. In contrast, when I leave Italy, my language acquisition quickly drops off, despite my best efforts to keep studying. Book learning is important, but it's just not the same.

Immersion makes your brain pay attention.

It's the same with programming your magical new life... it takes *immersing yourself* in positivity-focused actions, habits, and micro-rituals. Otherwise, you get distracted, and the whole process slows down. We don't want that.

Maintaining your elevated emotional state is important for two big reasons:

1) Keeping your emotions elevated makes you feel good all day long! Who doesn't want that? The people in your life will notice, too. It will even start to rub off on them.

2) Keeping the good feelings going as long as possible helps you make changes *faster*. You'll become the new you quicker and draw your future dreams closer.

This Daily Reader provides the little drips of daily self-love magic, self-worth glitter, and self-confidence power that you sip on all day. Or whenever you need a pick-me-up. Sometimes it's merely a thought you'll ponder, then move on. Another time, it might be just a fun way to think about life for that day. Other times, we'll dig a little deeper into our psyches to dig up gems we didn't even know were there.

But the total is more than the sum of these little drips. When you're done, you'll be equipped with a gilded, bedazzled tool belt, so when a certain thing happens, something less than ideal... you'll suddenly realize, *Oh, I have a tool for this. I know exactly how to respond, so I keep my vibe high! Yeehaw!*

Stress and fear turn off your heart's flow of love. But it's this love that helps you deal with stress and create a better life in which there is less stress in the first place. After reading this book, not only will you have a bunch of different ways to approach stress and reduce it, but you will also, in turn, possess a bunch of new ways to ramp up the love, happiness, and joy in your life.

Are You Ready?

I sail through my life with an over-the-top happiness that I feel in my bones. It keeps me calm and relaxed. Even if I have a choppy-water day, deep down in my core, I remain happy and secure.

It's an amazing feeling, but I wasn't always like this. I trained my brain for it. It's empowering, and I worked at it to get where I am today. Join me... *you can be like this, too!*

All my very best, and love to you,

Kristen

P.S. For a free, printable PDF with cut-out affirmations and fun reminders to hang on your refrigerator, email me at:

Kristen@HappySexyMillionaire.me

Please specify that you'd like the *"Daily Reader #1 Fridge Stuff."*

COFFEE SELF-TALK PRIMER

For Those Who Are New to Coffee Self-Talk

If you have recently read the book, *Coffee Self-Talk,* you can skip this brief section, unless you'd like a quick review.

For those of you who have not read *Coffee Self-Talk*, or who haven't read it in a while, I'll give you a brief overview. I won't go into all the details about positive self-talk, or how life-changing it can be, or why combining it with coffee creates a special kind of daily magic, because covering all that would take a book. A book that's already been written.

What Is Coffee Self-Talk?

Coffee Self-Talk is a powerful, five-minute program you do every morning while you drink your coffee (or other beverage). It's a special morning ritual with a specific task:

reading, thinking—or ideally, speaking out loud—scripts filled with specific words designed to rewire your brain, change your thoughts, your beliefs, your behavior, and your life. It also immediately makes you feel amazing, empowered, and happy.

The scripts you use could be written by you, selected from the scripts provided in the Coffee Self-Talk book, or a combination of the two. Many people start with the scripts I provided, and then modify them. People's scripts also change over time, as they progress, or their priorities or life situation changes.

Coffee Self-Talk boosts your confidence and helps you realize your dreams, manifest your goals, and attract the life you've always wanted. It adds more sparkle into your life, more shiny love, more empowerment, and deeper satisfaction. And, importantly, it creates feelings of whole-ness, worthiness, and self-love. This last bit is extremely important. Without a sense of self-worth, you're not likely to reach many of your goals because, deep down, you won't feel like you deserve them, and your subconscious mind will sabotage your plans. Coffee Self-Talk is a fun, easy way to fix all that, and get you fired up, shimmering, and sparkling, like you've always deserved.

You are already magical! You always have been! Coffee Self-Talk brings that magic to the surface, where you can wield it to design the life of your dreams.

HOW TO USE THIS DAILY READER

As I mentioned in the preface, this book is not meant to replace your daily Coffee Self-Talk routine. This book is for the five-minutes *after* your Coffee Self-Talk time.

This book contains 30 "days"—thoughts, ideas, tips, tricks, and activities to amplify the effectiveness of your Coffee Self-Talk ritual.

These are things that have helped me personally to reduce stress and anxiety, and help me live my magical, happy life. I do them regularly.

Each day is meant to take about five minutes to complete. Some days may take a bit longer. For instance, if you opt to take notes or jot down your thoughts in a notebook or journal, or if the day has an exercise you want to spend a little more time on. It's all up to you.

As this is a "daily" reader, I expect most people will only read one unit per day. You can go through them sequentially, or skip around if you like. If you want to do more than one day at a time, please feel free... though I'd caution against doing too much all at once, as it may dilute the effectiveness. At some point, it's better to let what you've done sink in before moving on to do more.

Some of the days in this book will probably click with you immediately. As you work your way through the days, make a note in your notebook or journal, or simply highlight or bookmark those days that you find most helpful, and then refer back to them in the future, whenever the situation calls for it.

And if some of these techniques *really* resonate with you, you'll want to come back to them regularly. When you do this, they'll become ingrained in you, as part of your default go-to response when something happens in life that you need help navigating with grace. So, although the magic nuggets are bite-sized, and spaced out as one per day, don't be surprised if you find yourself coming back to a certain handful of them that you love.

The Exercises

Some of the days in this book contain exercises. Something small and uplifting, and they'll usually only take a few minutes to complete, unless you want to expand upon them. I recommend that you do the exercises. Not only to get the most of out of this book, but also to have fun!

On some days, I may ask you to pull up your smart phone's calendar, or your to-do list, or your notebook or journal, if you're using one. And some of the exercises will involve sticky notes (or scraps of paper and tape... whatever you have). On "sticky note days," if time permits, you might want to get creative with your color pens, and possibly stickers, for extra flair. I decorate mine elaborately. Seriously, I go nuts.

All right. Let's get started.

DAY 1: WAVE YOUR MAGIC WAND

Ester asked why people are sad. "That's simple," says the old man. "They are the prisoners of their personal history. Everyone believes that the main aim in life is to follow a plan. They never ask if that plan is theirs or if it was created by another person. They accumulate experiences, memories, things, other people's ideas, and it is more than they can possibly cope with. And that is why they forget their dreams."

— PAULO COELHO, *THE ZAHIR*

Life, by Design

Who do you want to be?

If you were truly living a life of your own design, what would you do with your entire day, from the moment you wake in the morning until you go to sleep?

What would your flow and energy be like?

Get out your magic wand. Use one of your colorful pens, if you like. Wave it in front of you and let your imagination run wild. You can be anyone you want, have anything you want. Imagine the totality of possibilities. What life would you choose? What would you do every day? What would be your purpose? What would life mean to you?

No limitations here. Don't color inside the lines... *there are no lines in this exercise.* Don't hide who you are. Shine, shine, shine! Let your mind go beyond any thoughts of "it can't happen" or "it won't work," because this magic wand *is magic.* Fairy godmother stuff. Because you are infinite. You are limitless! You get to go for whatever you want, or become whomever you choose to be, because that's your birthright. You're golden. You're amazing. You are here to live and play at the highest level. You're creating a new world for yourself, and a new you!

Be bold!

Your beautiful, inspired dreams are possible!

Ask Yourself These Questions

Take a moment to ponder each one, and come up with a serious answer. Feel free to write them down, but it's not required. What's important is that you take each question seriously, and give it a real answer.

Ok. If you had a magic wand:

- What time would you wake up each day?

- How would you feel when you wake up? Calm? Unhurried? Buzzing with energy?
- How would you move? How would you stand?
- What would you do when you got out of bed?
- How would you spend your day?
- Is there a part of you that you need to heal? Physically? Emotionally?
- Would you dance around your house?
- How much money would you have in your bank account? Why?
- Who would you spend time with?
- What would you do for work?
- What would you do for play?
- Where would you travel?
- What would you do more of?
- What would you do less of?
- *What would your life be like?*

Isn't this fun?

Now take a moment and think about the answers you came up with. When you contemplate them, do you see a common thread running through them? Is there a *theme*? Perhaps a theme of abundance? Or freedom? Or love? Or adventure? Or just plain fun? Or a mix of these?

In other words... what do you *really* want when you dig down and get at the underlying desire behind the things you'd use your magic wand for? For example, if it's a new job you want, well, you don't just want a new job... there's a reason for it. What is that reason? Security? Autonomy? Respect? A shorter commute? A chance to work with great people? Or to work on something meaningful? Or challenging?

Is the reason money? If so, why? What would you do with the money?

Whether it's a new job you'd use your magic wand for, or something else, keep asking the question *"Why?"* for each item on your list, and drill down to the essence of why you want these things.

Is it freedom you ultimately seek? Is it abundance? Or maybe it's all about love, and everything in your magic-wand dream life is about love, nurturing, and generosity. Maybe it's a desire to be more spiritual and communing every day with something larger than yourself.

Pick a word that sums up the major theme. Some common themes are freedom, success, creativity, recognition, love, generosity, and abundance.

The first time I did this exercise, my initial answers mostly revolved around money. Not because I obsess about money, but because I already had health and beautiful relationships, and so financial independence was sort of the next thing on my hierarchy of desires.

But when I dug deeper, it fascinated me to realize that what I was really after... was *freedom*. Freedom to do what I want, to set my own schedule, to not have to answer to anybody. It was kind of there the whole time—hidden in plain sight—with the *independence* part of "financial independence." It literally means "financial *freedom*," yet I'd never made that connection until I scrutinized my reasons for wanting wealth.

So now, when I do this exercise, I skip right past money and concentrate on the word *freedom*. And I close my eyes and imagine a pair of purple and blue glittery wings in my mind. I visualize it over and over, to anchor the symbol (wings) to the thing that I actually want: freedom.

By focusing on freedom, my own magic-wand visualization exercise incorporates money in ways I hadn't considered. For instance, previously, visualizing wealth might have involved the idea of owning multiple homes. But is that really freedom? Not when a water pipe breaks, and you're not there. Vacation rentals might offer a lot more freedom, if that's what I'm really after.

But equally important is the feeling that comes with the word *freedom*. It's powerfully uplifting for me. This encourages more opportunities to feel the elevated emotions that help me manifest exactly what I'm seeking and attracting.

Did you come up with a theme word (or words) that summarize what it is that you really seek? If not, ponder this until you've come up with some candidates. Chew on it for a while.

If you want to apply a little pressure to yourself, imagine you have this magic wand, *but you only get to use it one time.* So you'd better make it count. What life would you create?

And if you already know your theme word, jot it down on a sticky note, and put it someplace really important, where you'll see it multiple times per day. For me, that's on my laptop. And keep this sticky of yours there for at least four weeks (unless you change your mind about your theme).

Why four weeks? That's long enough for the theme word to become a regular feature in your daily routine. It will be impossible for you to forget. It'll have done its job. Longer than four weeks, and the sticky's effectiveness will start to diminish, as you'll have become habituated to its presence. At that time, if you still need to remind yourself about your theme, then create a new sticky with that word, on a different colored note, and put it in a different location. Repeat as needed.

You wield magic!

～

Today's affirmation:

I am excited about the dream life I'm designing.

DAY 2: FINDING YOUR BLISS TIME

"Do not set aside your happiness. Do not wait to be happy in the future. The best time to be happy is always now."

— ROY T. BENNETT

I hear it all the time:

"I'd love to do Coffee Self-Talk every morning, but... five minutes? Every morning? Where am I going to find five minutes?!"

Wow.

I mean, I sort of get it. Sure, some people have a hard time taking five minutes out of their morning. Even for their own self-improvement. They claim it's hard to find the time. Maybe you have small children at home, and you're covered in smashed peas. Maybe you have a crazy schedule, with a job that requires an hour commute each way, or kids that need to be driven to school. Maybe you're running a small business. Or have a lot of responsibility at work. Or maybe you're busy on social media, or watching Netflix, or continuously refreshing your email.

It doesn't matter what your reason or excuse is. If you want to live *your greatest, most magical life ever*, you're going to have to make some time for YOU.

If you want to shine bright, like the shimmery being you were meant to be, you need to take care of yourself. It starts with small steps.

The easiest step is to wake up five minutes earlier. That's it. Get up and love yourself. That's what I did. Back in the day, when I was beginning my transformation, I knew I'd make excuses, or need to tend to my family, and I wouldn't take the time I deserved. So, in the beginning, I set my alarm for five minutes earlier than usual, to give myself what I call my special "Bliss Time."

Bliss Time

After a couple of weeks of waking to my alarm, five minutes earlier than before, I became more confident about taking charge of my schedule and observing how beneficial my time was for my self-improvement. And funny thing, when my family saw the changes in my mood and behavior, they were more than happy to give me the time I wanted. As a happier mom and wife, everybody in the house was happier. As my husband says, *happy wife, happy life.* (A 2014 Rutgers University study found that this old saying is basically true.) Your positivity is contagious!

Your mission is to carve out your own special Bliss Time. The best way to do this is to structure your life in a way that makes it happen automatically. Like brushing your teeth and eating food. You never forget to do those, right? Self-care and self-love time are *essential* if you want to live a magical life. Required. Not optional. To make this behavior become automatic, you need to focus some of your self-talk around the idea of making it *easy* to take time for yourself.

Today's exercise is designed to put you into a mindset that makes it easier to find time for yourself. You have *permission* to do this, to carve out five minutes just for you— every day. It's *important*. It's a new *priority*. Call it that. Say it out loud: *"My Bliss Time is a priority."*

If you didn't say it, then stop reading right now, and say it out loud (if possible).

My Bliss Time is a priority.

Staking your claim to five minutes every day will boost your confidence about taking better care of yourself in general. This claiming of five minutes—from here on out —is an action you can take that screams, *"I am worth it! I want a better life!"*

With that in mind, here's today's exercise. Ready? Ok. Here we go.

Step one:

Say to yourself (out loud, if possible), *"I care about how I feel."*

Now say it again.

Say it a third time, with some warmth, some feeling behind the words.

Step two:

Say, *"I am worthy of taking time for my own precious self-love, because I am precious."*

Say it again.

Say it a third time, feeling deep in your heart how wonderful and worthy you are of this time for yourself. Your Bliss Time.

Step three:

Read the following script out loud:

I care about how I feel.

I am worthy of taking time for my own precious self-love, because I am precious.

I love taking time for my own personal growth.

I'm making my dreams come true by taking time for me.

I have fun with my self-love time.

I love my "me time" because it elevates my spirit.

I love being kind to myself.

I make time for me.

Your Turn to Play!

Get out three sticky notes and your phone (or to-do list/calendar/notebook/etc.). On your sticky notes, write, "*I make time for me.*"

Then get your phone (etc.) and add the same line some-place where you'll see it a few times during the day (such as a calendar event, or to-do item with a reminder). If you're doing this exercise in the morning, setting your reminders for the afternoon and evening is a good idea.

Next, take your written sticky notes and put them some-place you're sure to see them... bathroom mirror, refriger-ator, nightstand, etc.

Every time you see these, say what you wrote two times, to yourself or out loud. (Or five times for extra oomph.)

Then, smile. :)

You are beautiful. You deserve five minutes every day.

Today's affirmation:

I make time for me.

DAY 3: OPEN TO RECEIVE!

"Whoever is happy will make others happy."

— ANNE FRANK

"I'm open to receive. I'm open to receive. I'm open to receive!"

That's me, walking around Rovigo, Italy, a couple of years ago, telling the universe to send me whatever it wants, because, hey, *I'm open to receive*. I was saying this out loud as I walked through the town. The people on the street didn't know what I was saying... they only spoke Italian.

It's like opening the doors to a new business and shouting from the rooftop, "I'm open for business!" If you don't, how will people know you're there? So tell the universe you're open for business, so it knows you're ready to play ball.

The first couple of times I said this out loud, it felt weird. I had to fake it, force it, and it made me wonder, *Why is this so hard?*

Oh, yeah. That whole worthiness thing.

Did I feel unworthy? I mean, deep down?

For the whole *receive from the universe* thing to work, I first had to believe I was worthy to receive. But at the time, I was still wearing my *I am worthy* training wheels. I didn't always feel it. But I knew I wanted to. I knew it was the foundation to manifesting my magical dream life. I reminded myself of the old line,

Fake it till you make it.

So I faked it. I said, "I am worthy to receive," even though I didn't completely believe it. And I kept saying it, over and over. And it soon got easier. And I could feel myself getting emotionally stronger, and I felt more worthy every day.

And before I knew it, I wasn't faking it anymore. I really did feel worthy and open to receive.

And I still do, over two years later.

It's time for you to open your hands and heart and be open to receiving all the gifts you're meant to receive. Open your hands, train your mind to attract, receive, and *accept* help and gifts of all kinds. Not just those you seek, but also those that you never even imagined. (I often imagine a gilded box, with a shimmering red bow on my porch right outside my door, thinking that the universe is always stopping by with gifts for me.)

Your Turn to Play!

Sit comfortably in a quiet place. Dim the lights, if you like.

Close your eyes, and imagine a gilded box, with a shimmering, red bow, placed directly in front of you. Take a deep breath, and slowly speak the words,

> *I am worthy to receive. I am open to receive.*

Repeat it ten times. Then, imagine yourself lifting the lid off the box. As you do, a brilliant, white light bursts out of the box, swirling and sparkling around you in a dazzling light show. Imagine the light entering you and warming your heart.

You can do this simple visualization any time you like, to give you confidence and reinforce what is already true...

You are worthy and open to receive.

$\sim$

Today's affirmation:

I am worthy to receive everything my heart desires.

DAY 4: LOVING THE CRACKS

"There is nothing more rare, nor more beautiful, than a woman being unapologetically herself, comfortable in her perfect imperfection. To me, that is the true essence of beauty."

— STEVE MARABOLI

Life's flow can sometimes knock you sideways, or even way off course. You might look at these bumps in life with a stink-eye, a sour feeling in your stomach, or lose sleep, or even carry long-term scars. You might liken these scars to a bowl that breaks, and it's glued back together, functional, but no longer perfect.

But life's flow and bumps don't have to be viewed that way.

Life is forever changing. There are bumps, peaks, and valleys along your path. Changes happen, mistakes are made, but through these experiences, we can come out more beautiful than before.

Kintsugi

Kintsugi is the beautiful, centuries-old Japanese art of repairing broken pottery, where the artisans put the pieces back together, filling the cracks with a gorgeous, shimmering gold lacquer. The aesthetic embodies a philosophy built on the idea that, when you embrace flaws and imperfections, you are stronger and *more* beautiful. The breaks in these pieces of pottery tell a story of the piece's history, and they are deliberately highlighted with gold, prominent and proud. These works of art are so much more interesting than regular, unbroken pottery. Kintsugi treats imperfections as something to embrace. Not disguise. It's a spectacular way to look at failures, mistakes, and life's bumpity-bumps.

Imagine living that way! Looking at mistakes or failures as something beautiful to highlight with gold and sparkles. Maybe in the moment something goes wrong, you feel bad, but if you know that putting yourself back together, with love, will transform you into something more than you were before, highlighting—not hiding—the lessons. You're no longer a victim. You're not weakened by the challenges; you're strengthened and emboldened. You become something dazzling.

Realize this:

Perfection is not the goal.

The real beauty is in living life, learning, and loving yourself, all the way through the process. The totality of the experience: triumphs, failings, lessons, and gilded cracks.

All of it.

Your Turn to Play!

Take a moment to let this philosophy take root.

In the future, whenever you make a mistake or encounter bumps in the road, you can now see them as a source of beauty. They're part of what makes you interesting and unique. They are the spicy bits of the journey that's unfolding before you.

Now look back on your past, and do the same thing. Think of a mistake you've made, or something you see as an imperfection. It can be something big or small. It can be something physical, emotional, or anything. See it in this new light of kintsugi, and how it makes you a unique and beautiful creature. See how beautiful you are with all your life's experiences and everything you are, right now.

You are sublime.

~

Today's affirmation:

I am light. I shimmer gold... my past, my now, and my future. I am me. I love me.

DAY 5: RELEASING ON THE WINGS OF BUTTERFLIES

"There is only one way to happiness, and that is to cease worrying about things that are beyond the power of our will."

— EPICTETUS

Today, we dive into the beautiful process of *releasing*.

When you want to release a bad or harmful habit, you can incorporate a line about it into your Coffee Self-Talk. By adding a line that says, *Today, I release the need for* _____, and repeating it, and feeling how free and amazing it would be to let go of the need, you enter a powerful and elevated emotional experience.

It is within this experience that change occurs.

Even better, when you say this throughout your day, your brain will work extra hard to make it happen. Remember, your brain is always listening to everything you say and think. It is looking for direction and guidance from you. *It wants you to tell it what to do.* So when you repeatedly direct your brain to release the need for something, you simply wake up one day and no longer feel the need for it.

You can use this technique for pretty much anything... releasing the need for a certain food, or alcohol, or a behavior like gossiping, or showing up late to things. Or you can release the feeling of jealousy, or the need to be perfect, or the need to criticize others, or the need to criticize yourself. Or the need to complain. Or release the need to worry about something specific, like your health, for example. Or the need to worry about wrinkles.

Butterflies to the Rescue!

Sometimes, when I'm repeating the affirmation of something I want to release (or many things!), I picture myself sitting outside in a chair, and in my imagination, it's a beautiful, sunny day. The sky is a vibrant blue, and there are trees all around, leaves rustling in the gentle breeze. Next to my chair is a table, and on this table stands an endless line of monarch butterflies, and they're waiting for me.

The first butterfly steps up close to me. I tell the little butterfly what I want to release. For example,

I release the need to criticize myself.

When I say this, I imagine the need inside of me coming out and softly landing on the wings of the waiting butterfly. And then, the butterfly takes off and flies away, carrying with it my need to criticize. Up, up, and away, fluttering gently, as only a butterfly can do. I'm left feeling lighter.

The next butterfly walks up, I repeat the words, and he flies away. And on and on. I'll do this for a couple of minutes, until the need is fully released. It's so powerful!

Your Turn to Play!

If you're not already seated, sit down someplace quiet. Think of something you want to stop doing, and then write down, *I release the need for* _____ (fill in the blank).

For now, only focus on one thing to release, and repeat the mental exercise I described above, with five to ten butterflies.

Feel the lightness you'd feel with the need released and permanently gone. And then smile, knowing that your brain is listening and going to work on doing exactly what you tell it.

You are magical.

∽

Today's affirmation:

When I'm already in a state of worthiness, gratitude, and empowerment, I feel like my desires have already come true.

DAY 6: OOOF! DAYS

"Stop comparing yourself to other people, just choose to be happy, and live your own life."

— ROY T. BENNETT

You know those days when things just go wrong? Like the time my husband locked the keys to his friend's car inside the car.

In the middle of the street.

With the engine running.

OOOF!

Or when you're baking cupcakes for a birthday party, and you realize you're out of an ingredient, so you have to go to the store? *Three times?*

OOOF.

What can you do when you have a day that's *OOOF?* What

should you do if, one day, your emotions are in the gutter? Or you just can't get your shit together?

First, it's normal, and it's not a problem to have a day like this. No worries! It can happen for several reasons: hormones, a pile of things that finally just poke you too hard, not enough self-love, your cup is overflowing (see Day 29), Mercury is in retrograde, or anything.

These are OOOF days, because when they happen, you just go *OOOF!* If you have a day like this, the most important thing is that you not worry. Next, you recognize it and be aware of it. When you recognize an OOOF day (or an OOOF moment)... pat yourself on your back. *You're self-aware!* Bravo! You're no longer going through life unconscious of your mental state. You're paying attention!

So, the first thing you do when you recognize it, is you say to yourself, "Ah, I'm having an OOOF day." No emotion, just an observation.

The next step is to recover your regular magical self, and get back up on that glorious, flying Pegasus of yours. (See tips, below!) When you do this, you'll quickly regain your shimmer, get back to your new habits, and the new you that you've been creating. You'll also see that your brain and heart learn on days like this. It's fascinating... you actually get faster and faster at returning to that blissful state each time you have an *OOOF!* Day. You become an expert at *recapturing your groove.* So, yes, moments of ooof-ness can come, but they don't last! Celebrate that.

Ways to Regain Your Sparkle on OOOF! Days

First, give yourself a good ol' fashioned break. Be gentle with yourself and say, *"OK, this is a choppy-water day. No big deal. I got this."*

Options to navigate the mental whitecaps:

1. Take a break, and do something you enjoy (Netflix, ice cream, music, a bubble bath, sex, spa day, peanut butter, doing nothing but staring at the wall, anything you enjoy). Doing these things will inject instant joy into your life, for three reasons:

- It'll add more deep love for yourself, because you are taking care of yourself.
- You're recognizing your own needs, which makes you more powerful. And...
- Well, Netflix and ice cream, right? Doing things we enjoy is... wait for it... *enjoyable.*

2. Pick one line of your Coffee Self-Talk and repeat it like a mantra all *freakin'* day. You'll say it so much that it'll become almost mindless as you do it, and that's ok. This puts you in a bit of a trance, which helps you just kinda float through the day on fluffy, lavender clouds.

On an *OOOF!* Day, my favorite line of self-talk I repeat to myself is,

I am worthy I am worthy I am worthy I am worthy I am worthy I am worthy—repeatedly—*I am worthy I am worthy I am worthy. IamworthyIamworthyIamworthy!*

Even as you read it here, the words almost start to lose their meaning (it's called *semantic fatigue*)... and I don't care. I'm gonna pound these words into my brain until I'm a brainwashed, worthy-ass robot. I say it while washing dishes. I say it while cooking. I say it while taking out the trash. I say it while taking off my shoes. I say it while starting the car. I say it while walking to the bathroom. I say it while on the toilet, peeing. I say it while brushing my teeth (garbled, foam flying from my mouth like Cujo). I say it as I fall asleep. I say it... all *OOOFing* day long.

3. Take a walk! (Do not skip reading this one.) A super-duper effective way to reset your mindset is to take a walk. It doesn't matter if it's a loop you do ten times in your driveway, up-n-down your street, or circling your yard, because going outside for fresh air will invigorate your soul, like jump starting a battery in a car. (No matter the weather! If it's cold, dress warm, people! If it's raining, take an umbrella. No excuses.) Put on your tennis shoes, and go out for a walk. It'll help you get your groove back much faster.

4. Lean into love, and know you are safe, seen, and supported. Sometimes it's a simple matter of leaning into thoughts of love for yourself, for your *OOOF!* Day, and knowing that you're seen and supported by all the other Coffee Self-Talkers out there, myself included. If you have an OOOF! Day, you can close your eyes and send out a silent call to us, and we'll send you energy of love. Or hop over to the private Coffee Self-Talk Facebook group. It's filled with epically awesome people sharing their love, kindness, and support with each other. Some of the things

I see and read in there bring tears to my eyes, they're so beautiful.

5. Take the day and focus your love on the itty-bitty-teeny-tiny things in your life... like your cup of coffee... *I love you, coffee*. Water, *I love you, water*. Roof, *I love you, roof over my head*. Pretty toenail polish, *I love you, pretty toenail polish*. Sun, *I love you, sun*. Wine cooler... *I love you, wine cooler*. Toilet paper... *I love you, toilet paper*.

All day long... by telling things you love that you love them, you'll immediately feel gratitude and put things into perspective. It'll also keep the love flowing by keeping your mind occupied with love instead of fear, or stress, or just plain grumpiness. It keeps your elevated emotions at play and snuffs out the ooofness.

Poof!

You are triumphant!

～

Today's affirmation:

I am strong and confident. I'm full of love. I believe in me.

DAY 7: NEW PERSPECTIVE HAT

"Happiness is what makes you pretty. Period. Happy people are beautiful. They become like a mirror, and they reflect that happiness."

— DREW BARRYMORE

Today, we're going to change it up and do something that will make you feel a bit more fresh and invigorated. Today is a day for another perspective, wearing a different "hat" in your life, which is fun (and helpful!), because having different perspectives shows us there is more than one way to do things, or think about things.

Holding multiple perspectives opens our minds, and when that happens, our ego is suppressed, which boosts creativity and mindfulness. It can even be exhilarating and adventurous!

I call it "wearing the New Perspective Hat." There are many ways for you to wear it. It could be trying something new, such as a food, drink, or outfit. It could be trying a new restaurant, visiting a new park, or a museum. It can mean meeting new people, changing your path to work, using your non-dominant hand (see Day 22). Or trying a new recipe for dinner. Instead of using salt, maybe you use soy sauce. Switch the side of the bed you sleep on tonight. Take a shower by candlelight. Have a kid teach you a video game. Or jump on a trampoline.

How about this one? Download a new app or game to your phone today. Or learn some new words in another language! Like this... pick out five words you use in your everyday language, go to Google Translate, translate them into another language. Then use those words today, every chance you get. *Meravigliosa!* (Marvelous!)

These are all lovely little micro ways for you to try out a new perspective today. Pick one or many! As you imagine these new things you can do, they become like mini-goals for the day, and when our brain knows we're setting out to accomplish something, it creates a happy chemical in our brain called dopamine. So, not only is this activity beneficial for opening our minds, it will also give you a legit bump in the happiness chemicals inside you. In short, it'll make you feel good.

You could even don a bigger perspective hat... like planning a trip somewhere you've never been, or trying a new sport or hobby. New experiences like this stimulate the growth of new brain cells and generate excitement in your life, new opportunities, and exploded creativity. They also make you more mindful because your brain pays attention to new things. In fact, it's pretty much impossible to be mindless when attempting something new that excites you.

As I write this, in the midst of the COVID pandemic in 2021, I'm currently living in a small, medieval hilltop town in Italy. We don't have a car, and we don't do public transportation due to the pandemic, so everything I do is on foot. With these limited options for travel and meeting people, when I put on my "New Perspective Hat" lately, I simply take a different route to the grocery store. One time, on one of these new routes, I bought cheese from a cheesemaker's shop I discovered, instead of the grocery store.

These examples may seem silly and insignificant, but you'd be amazed at the new sparkle something like this can add to your day, or heck, your life. By the third time I walked into the cheese shop, the owner started smiling and calling me by name, even though she didn't speak a word of English. It's not a huge thing, and it's a limited interaction, due to social distancing, masks, and the language barrier, but this little exchange never fails to brighten my day. All because I walked a different route one day.

There's a beautiful trail that goes all the way around our hilltop village, a three-mile loop, offering spectacular views of the rolling hills and valley surrounding us. I walk it almost every day for my exercise, and I'd always walk the same direction on the trail. Habit, I suppose. Well, one day, I changed it up, just for the hell of it. I put on my New

Perspective Hat, and I walked the trail in the opposite direction.

I chuckle about it... you're probably thinking, *"big deal, Kristen."* But it turned out to be a huge deal, because I saw so many things I'd never seen before. They had been literally hidden from my eyes when I only went the one way: flowers, trees, views, little alcoves, and new views of the surrounding countryside.

All right there, the whole time, and I never even knew it!

We are creatures of habit. Break those habits, just for a day. Flip your day around, and be in awe of the difference it makes.

Your Turn to Play!

What is something you can do differently today? Plan it, and do it. If you're up for it, do more than one new thing. Next step is marking your calendar once a month for a "New Perspective Hat" day, so you can do this fun exercise regularly.

You are a beautiful and creative genius!

Today's affirmation:

I love learning new things and going on new adventures. Yesss!

DAY 8: HAND ON HEART MOMENT

"*I felt my lungs inflate with the onrush of scenery—air, mountains, trees, people. I thought, 'This is what it is to be happy.*'"

— SYLVIA PLATH

Your heart is where your true power comes from.

Our brains come up with ideas, and our hearts provide the feelings and reactions to those ideas. Your heart gives your ideas energy!

(Technically, emotions live in the brain's limbic system, but it *feels like the heart*, so let's stick with that metaphor.)

You want your thoughts and feelings to be united. For example, when your brain comes up with a brilliant idea, you don't want your heart holding you back with the emotion of fear. You want to be excited about the idea! You want to be inspired to take action. Ideas are nothing without energy. Your brain is nothing if your heart isn't pulling in the same direction.

Your heart being in sync with your brain is the source of confidence. You feel certainty, because you're not at war with yourself. You feel calm, even in a storm.

And this is why, when we have great thoughts and great feelings, we live a more magical life. We manifest our dreams faster. We live leagues happier. In the moment, and in the future.

With this in mind, let's talk about your beautiful heart. Let's revere in how your heart fuels your ideas with powerful energy. The heart is the seat of your soul, it's your wholeness, your worthiness. It's your love. *It's you.*

Your connection to yourself, to everybody else, and to your magic, your energy... comes from your heart. Your greatest opportunities lie in the power of the loving energy you can tap into, that feeling right in the center of your chest, when you know you're *doing the right thing.*

Go ahead and place your hand on your heart, right now, as you're reading this.

From this magnificent center in your body, right under-neath your hand in the center of your chest, is where joy, abundance, worthiness, love, and wholeness swirl, ready for you to manifest your dreams. It's your *life.* You know the feelings I'm talking about, because you've had them before. Whenever something wonderful happens, or you're super grateful, or wildly excited about something, or your mind is blown in awe, there's an incredible energy dazzling in your chest. Sometimes it feels so powerful that you almost feel like your chest is cracking open, and love is pouring out. You might even cry.

You want to feel this a lot.

Like, *a lot* a lot.

You want to feel this feeling as often as you can. And there are ways to do that. You draw from your experience. Think of a time when you had this feeling... perhaps your marriage proposal, or learning you were going to have a baby, or witnessing the birth of a child. Or maybe you witnessed something wonderful in nature, like elephants banding together to help another elephant out of the mud, or maybe you observed pure generosity between two strangers, or sacrifices people make for others, which show you the power of love.

Or maybe you heard a testimonial about someone doing something epic, or the recounting of a tale that stirs your core. Or scenes in a movie, or part of a song, and you feel a rumbling thunder in your chest as energy builds up, wanting to burst out! Or simply looking at an ocean's rolling surf, or a blazing sunset, or the night sky filled with a billion stars, hinting at the vastness of possibility!

Experiences like these fuel this beautiful radiance in your chest. *That's* the feeling you want!

Now, if you can't quite conjure up the feeling yet, then you can imagine it. Imagine an epic, swirling, life-force energy, like a superhero using his or her superpower. In your mind, give this glistening energy a color, give it a form, and imagine how incredible it would feel to have it swirling all around you like a dazzling, shimmering cyclone.

So! Your mission, should you choose to accept it, is to practice imagining this feeling enough times that you anchor it, and you can tap into it anytime.

To do this, you want to become mindful of your emotions, all day. That is, pay attention to your feelings. Without judgement. Just notice them. And when something great happens, or you experience an unexpected wave of self-love during your Coffee Self-Talk (this happens *all* the time), remember it. Anchor the feeling. Drink it in, guzzle it, chew on it.

Then, throughout the day, draw it up in your mind, and cue it up in your heart, and bathe in the elevated emotion that swirls and twirls through you, and all around you.

Your Turn to Play!

Have a seat. Put your hand over your heart and feel your heartbeat, thumping magnificently under your palm. Close your eyes, take a deep breath, and feel the amazing energy. Give your heart thanks. *"Thank you, beautiful heart, for beating for me, all this time."* (Sometimes, I do a few jumping jacks first to make it beat faster, and I can really feel it thumping through my chest.)

Relax, and let yourself drift through these elevated emotions of gratitude for your heart, and awe that it beats and beats and beats, pumping love through you every minute of your life. Take this energy with you into your day.

Write *"Hand Over Heart"* on one sticky note, and draw a heart around the words. Place it on your bathroom mirror.

Every time you see the note, take a deep breath, put your hand over your heart, give it thanks, and draw in an elevated emotion.

You are the embodiment of love.

Today's affirmation:

Wholeness is inside me and all around me. My color shines and lights up my life.

DAY 9: MICRO-UPGRADES FOR A LIFE OF ABUNDANCE

"Money may not buy happiness, but I'd rather cry in a Jaguar than on a bus."

— FRANÇOISE SAGAN

"I'll take the ribeye," I boldly declared one day at the butcher. I normally bought the cheaper ground beef.

Another day, I bought the beautiful, fresh *buffalo mozzarella* balls that I usually passed on. Oh, and that time I went for the organic dried blueberries! Those were a treat.

These are examples of times I gave myself permission to get a little taste (literally and figuratively) of the life I'd live if I had paid off my debt and was making a lot of money— I opted to buy something I wouldn't normally buy because of the cost. I wanted to take a sip from the flow of abundance that, in my heart, I knew was coming my way. Like a micro-upgrade. A small, confident wink *from me* to the universe that I was playing ball with her. I was dipping my toe into the experience of doing things I'd do if I were financially wealthy.

These little treats would allow me to feel the elevated emotion of abundance. I was excited about it!

But as I walked to the butcher shop with my intention, I had a moment of trepidation. I wondered if I was being irresponsible. Wouldn't it make more sense to eat ground beef to save money? Wouldn't that take me closer to my goal? Every dollar saved would go straight to paying off the credit card.

Prior to this time, I'd taken my family down a severely frugal path, in which I even calculated the cost per gram of protein and analyzed my spending to the penny, in my desperate attempt to get out of debt. And it helped, to a point—such as eliminating frivolous costs. But beyond that, I was mostly just driving myself crazy. I became obsessed, a little nuts even, to the point of not wanting to run our air conditioning in the Arizona summer, which actually impaired our productivity and ability to generate income. All I did 24 hours a day was stew in the survival emotions of scarcity and lack. Constant *fear*. And it affected my husband and daughter. My *lack* mentality was contagious, and it hung over our home like a dark, stormy cloud.

But that extreme behavior was in the past. Since then, I'd acquired a more balanced perspective, more *mindful* than knee-jerk frugality, scrimping when it made sense, but also spending when it made sense.

And occasionally, I would splurge. *Mindfully.*

I realized at that moment, walking to the butcher, that there's a delicate balance, a dance, between smart frugality and attracting abundance. If your frugality comes from a growth mindset, and not fear, then it can be a wealth attractor. But if your frugality comes from a scarcity mindset, it can send your subconscious mind a powerful message that you live in scarcity, or that you're not worthy, and it hampers your attempts to manifest wealth.

I wanted to make my intentions very clear. Both to myself, and to the universe. So I indulged with a nice ribeye once in a while. I chose this, and other *micro-abundance* options (i.e., under $20), and I did it with confidence. Gusto, even!

Dr. Joe Dispenza teaches that you can't live in a scarcity mindset, with low-vibration emotions such as lack, and then expect prosperity to rain down in gold coins. It's important that you *feel abundant* in order to draw abundance. Like Dr. Joe says,

> *"Abundance is tied to a frequency of worthiness and freedom, which carry the message or intent of your individual desire for wealth."*

And so, get this! Because the universe likes to wink back, a week later, the most amazing synchronicity occurred. I heard a podcast with a woman telling a story similar to mine, about indulging herself in small ways. And she chose *blueberries!* Not the frozen bag, but the expensive fresh ones in the small container. For the same reason— she wanted to sample the taste of abundance.

I was blown away!

I mean... freakin' blueberries? What are the odds? (See Day 12, *Seeing Synchronicities*.) This wink back from the universe boosted my confidence. *I was on the right track!*

Now, I didn't immediately go and start booking first-class tickets for our next flight... though I admit, it did cross my mind, hehe. Instead, I stayed the course, going with the wiser, micro-abundance pleasures: more occasional ribeyes, the fancy cheese balls, and more blueberries. Instead of always working from home, as I'd done during my freaky-frugal days, once a week, I started tasting the micro-abundance of a wonderful cafe, working there on my laptop, drinking cappuccinos and getting hot chocolate and croissants for my daughter.

It's true, I paid down a big chunk of debt living frugally, but I took it too far, and it stressed the crap out of me and my family. Then I got smart about it and dialed things back. At which point, I immediately felt more relaxed about *everything*. I felt good about my choices, and I'd found a good balance between saving money and indulging in a few carefully chosen micro-upgrades to my life.

The Abundance Mindset

While we often associate "abundance" with money, there

are other ways to feel abundant, and therefore attract all kinds of abundance.

Abundance is a mindset that applies no matter what you seek—love, money, health, or anything else. You are the foundation for making your dreams come true. You are like the *on-off* switch. Turn it on with elevated emotions, and you'll see more connections, more solutions, more opportunities. Turn it off with negativity, fear, survival, or grasping, and your ability to see all of these opportunities goes dark.

So, to keep attracting abundance of all kinds, it's essential to keep your feelings high and bright despite anything that's going on in your life. Remember, we all have challenges, but what sets the winners apart from everyone else is how they handle these challenges. How they handle their emotional state, such that they're better equipped to think and take action. Your thoughts make a difference! You have power! *We all do!*

Your daily Coffee Self-Talk routine trains you for this, every time you read your scripts. And the more practice you get, the more abundance you will attract, and the more magical your life will become.

Your Turn to Play!

The feeling of abundance starts in your mind and your heart. It might take practice if you've been spending most of your time stewing in the emotions of scarcity and lack, but the more you think about abundance coming to you, the more often you will actually *feel* the emotions of abundance.

A great way to start is with gratitude. No matter what kind of abundance you'd like (financial, love, energy, health, success, creative, etc.), stop and appreciate what you already have, so you can feel abundance at any time, no matter what's going on.

Think of all the stuff you have... the clothes on your back, the roof over your head, clean water, fresh air. The coffee you're drinking! You have so much abundance right now! At the same time, draw up your elevated emotions to really *feeeel* this appreciation, to bathe in your rich, sparkling abundance.

Next, write down five micro-upgrades—simple and inexpensive things you could have or do that pack so much concentrated joy that they'd make you feel like you had all you want or need. Examples might include:

- Taking a bath
- Doing your nails
- Buttered toast
- Fancy ice cream
- Taking a nap
- *Blueberries!*

Once you've created your list, select one of them, and indulge yourself! Be sure to fully luxuriate in the experience. Draw it out, if applicable. For example, if your indulgence is fancy ice cream, even just a single bite can be *amazing* if you close your eyes and *really* experience it. You don't need to *overindulge* to indulge!

And know that, in that moment of melting deliciousness, you're living a *magical moment* and drawing your *magical life* closer.

You are limited by nothing!

Today's affirmation:

Abundance is all around me and within me. It's everywhere I look.

DAY 10: THE MAGIC OF GOOD POSTURE

"Happiness is a state of activity."

— ARISTOTLE

"Shoulders back, tits out!"

I remember my mom saying this to me constantly when I was growing up. *"Don't slouch!"* she'd bark. I'm glad she was adamant about my having good posture ever since I was a kid. It has paid off for me. If you haven't made proper posture a priority, start today. It's never too late. It really makes a big difference in your mental and physical energy. Like, huge.

Why Are We Focusing on Posture Today?

So many reasons.

Good posture has so many benefits... it even helps you manifest your dreams faster. (More on that below.)

1) You'll instantly have more energy and more confidence, because when you slouch, you drain your energy. But when you go from slouching to sitting, or standing nice and tall, you'll notice an immediate boost in energy. This short-term energy increase is partly psychological, as we subconsciously associate sitting up straight with being more alert. When we're tired, we slouch, and thus slouching sends a message to the brain that we're at rest. In contrast, when we're more alert, we tend to sit up straight, which tells our brain to be ready for action, and it gives us more energy. And proper posture uses your muscles more efficiently, which allows the body to use less energy, which prevents fatigue.

2) Super posture also displays a feeling of "I'm attentive" to whatever is going on with your surroundings, which actually makes you more attentive (try it right now, and you'll see what I mean). Someone with good posture looks confident. If you were a warrior, you'd be standing tall and strong. If you were a politician on the campaign trail, you'd do well to stand proud. If you were at a job interview, or trying to get the attention of someone you fancy, you would definitely want to appear confident to be noticed. Standing and sitting tall can make you appear more attractive... even slimmer, too.

Keep these mental pictures of important scenarios in mind, and then apply them during your routine days, even when you're alone. It will make you feel more confident in the moment, as well as start building the habit so that you do it in public without thinking about it.

But here's where it gets really cool...

3) Good posture can help you *manifest your dreams and goals.*

What? You can reach your goals by... sitting up straight?

Absolutely! I call it the *Magic of Good Posture.* Apart from boosting your confidence and giving you more energy, as described above, you'll also tap into the reserve of elevated emotions that always exist inside you, but sometimes seem hard to access. Body position and movement are one of the ways to access that reserve.

And you want as many of those feel-good vibes as you can get. Plus... it can bring you more opportunities because *your* state changes *other people's* states.

Have you ever noticed how some people walk into a room and everyone notices and immediately feels uplifted because that person just exudes raw energy? When people are feeling great, living their dream, they simply show it with their body language.

And it's never slouching.

When you see this person, you're also drawn to him or her, and other people are, too. People want a taste of that magic he or she wields, that electric energy radiating from them. So imagine if that high-energy, confident person *was you* entering the room. Everyone wants to flock to you, everyone wants to be around you, everyone wants to work with you. And *that's* how opportunities rain down on you. Grab your umbrella, it's about to get wet.

Change your posture, change your life!

Your Turn to Play!

Today, pay attention to your posture and aim for *super posture*. Take stock of the way you breathe, the way you walk, the way you sit, the way you cook, the way you brush your teeth, the way you move. Even the way you speak and use your voice!

There are devices on the market that aim to train you to have good posture. I've not tried any of these, so I can't comment on their effectiveness, but they might be worth a look.

Reminders can be very helpful. Write "Super Posture!" on a few sticky notes and place then where you'll see them, including where you usually sit for long periods of time. Also set reminders on your phone.

Every time you see one of your reminder notes, or hear your phone's reminder, you're to stand (or sit) with good posture. If you were already sitting or standing straight, then pat yourself on your properly postured back!

Once you routinely have good posture, you'll start catching yourself anytime you *don't* have it, correcting yourself on the spot. In fact, you'll feel weird slouching and only feel comfortable with proper posture. The first time this happens, congratulate yourself. It means you have adopted the new habit. Poor posture will become the automatic trigger for good posture.

. . .

You are glorious!

Today's affirmation:

I stand tall, shoulders back, and face tipped to the sky. I am confidence. I am kindness. I am love.

DAY 11: THE EGO'S VACATION DAY

"I'd far rather be happy than right any day."

— Douglas Adams, *The Hitchhiker's Guide to the Galaxy*

Today, you're going to practice having no ego. And let me tell you... it feels *soooooo* nice. When your ego goes on vacation, it actually feels like a vacation for your soul. So let's pack your ego's little brown suitcase and send it on its way for a mini-getaway.

Now, having an ego is not always bad. You need it to survive. Aside from keeping you alive, the ego is also helpful in other ways.

For one thing, it helps define "you," as distinct from everything else, which is necessary for making sense of the world. It connects the *past* you to the *present* you, giving you the sense of having a personal history, and allows you to project an idea of that person into the future, which is necessary for planning and working toward goals.

The ego also gives you confidence and self-esteem when it comes from a place of love. Your ego is doing its job when you stand up for yourself. Or when you ask your boss for a raise. Or ask someone out on a date, or to marry.

Your ego can remind you that you're worthy of self-love.

And these are wonderful things.

But the darker side of the ego—the fragile part—is that it can give you angst and cause problems. It's the part that makes your heart crumple or lash out, because it's hurt. It can get out of control. And it's when the ego operates from fear that confidence turns to arrogance, in an attempt to protect itself.

The problem with the ego comes when it creates *any kind* of unnecessary survival emotion in you. The key word being "unnecessary," because fear can sometimes save you, such as prompting you to run when you're in physical danger. But the other times, the 99.99% of the times in your life that your ego makes you feel tightness, angst, unfairness, whiny, belittled, embarrassed, humiliated, slighted, excluded, unlucky, or a need to control or convince others... all of those times are not about survival, not in the modern world, anyway. They're about protecting your ego.

And these are perfectly normal, human emotions. Don't worry if you sometimes experience some of them.

But not today.

Today, you're going to send your ego on a vacation. Give it a little break. Some R&R.

What does this mean? It means, today, you have ZERO need for *praise*. And ZERO concern about *criticism*. Just for today, praise will not matter to you any more than it matters to a toaster. It will not boost your ego, nor make you feel better, nor validate your existence.

And on the flip side, criticism will also not matter. Regardless of what anybody says that's negative about you or anything you've ever done—or even if they just shoot you a look—today, you don't care. It will not make you feel bad. It will not make you question your abilities or worth. Not even 1%.

Why? Because your ego is gone. On some beach somewhere, sipping a piña colada.

Imagine your ego as a piece of furniture. This piece of furniture starts each day clean and free of dust. And then, throughout the day, dust falls on it, in the form of praise and criticism. These make your surface dirty, cloudy looking. If you didn't have the piece of furniture, the ego, there would be nowhere for the dust to fall. There would be no place for the praise or criticism to land. Without ego, there's nothing to bruise or hurt.

It would be like trying to punch an empty space. There's just nothing there.

That's the metaphor for today... your ego just... *isn't there.*

Don't worry, it can come back from vacation tomorrow, if you want it to.

In life, it's important to not let peoples' opinions or negative attitudes affect you emotionally. Note that this is different from learning; legitimate feedback from others may contain information that helps you learn and improve. None of which requires an emotional response... it's just data.

It's the *emotional* response to criticism that you want to train yourself to let go of.

But here's the less obvious part: You must also train your ego not to react emotionally to *praise*, either.

Come again? Surely, you're joking, Kristen. We like praise, right? It feels nice!

Nope, not joking. And yes, it does feel nice. Which is why we must learn to *ignore* that feeling.

You see, just as the ego can be cut down with criticism, it can also be built up with praise. And it feels so nice, that your nervous system can become dependent on it. Addicted. Needing constant praise to feel worthy, forever.

For this reason, you never want to *seek* praise, or become *attached* to praise. Again, this does not apply to the unemotional informational content of positive feedback. It also doesn't mean you don't want to do a good job. You do the good job because you do good work.

The more you love yourself, the less you will need praise from others to feel good about yourself. And the less you think about praise, the more you will love yourself. And so the cycle goes, round and round, until you arrive at a place with profound peace in your life.

Needing to Be Right

Aside from seeking praise from others, another thing that out-of-control egos often do is feel the need to be right.

Remember, your ego is on vacation today. Which means...

Today, you're going to let go of any and all need to defend your position on things. Let go of the longing to convince or persuade others. You can still hold on to your views without having to prove anything to others or justify your positions. Besides, research has shown that stubborn people are easier to persuade when you *don't* try to persuade them. Argumentation makes stubborn people dig in their heels—to defend *their* egos. (Stubbornness is always a sign of a fragile ego... *fear of being wrong.* Except with donkeys.) Instead, if you simply lay out the facts and shrug, and let the stubborn person go off and think, they are more likely to come to the new conclusion, believing they have done so on their own, thereby protecting their ego.

People are also more likely to change simply by witnessing your shining, happy example, rather than from your opinions.

When you free yourself from trying to change others, you actually get more clarity and freedom. And peace. The interesting thing to contemplate is that your views don't gain any validity or points when you defend them, nor do they lose any credibility when you choose not to defend them. You'll discover how powerful and simple it is to just relax, shrug it off, and to release the urge to defend yourself.

You may find that life without the ego is much more fun! With practice, it will happen! It's a liberating day, too, when you encounter a situation where your ego is quiet and relaxed. It doesn't get hyped up from others' praise, because you do that yourself with your own splendid self-talk. And it doesn't get its feathers ruffled from others' criticisms.

Note: The ego being on vacation doesn't mean you don't share your opinions, such as when it will help someone, or when you're asked. You're just not doing it to look good, or smart, or to be proven right.

Your Turn to Play!

Write *"No Ego Today"* on a couple of sticky notes, and place them where you'll see them. If you happen not to interact with people much today, you might want to post-pone your ego's vacation day for a time when you'll be more likely to see it in action.

Whether that's today or sometime in the future, enjoy the freedom of letting your ego take a day off. When you see one of your notes, let it remind you to say less today, defend less, and relax more.

And then tomorrow, when your ego is back to normal, see

if you can sense any difference. Did you feel more confident with or without the ego? Were you more effective? You may find that the answer is a bit of a mix. With mastery of your ego, you'll be able to turn it on and off at will, or dial it in to just the right amount, depending on the situation.

You are love.

～

Today's affirmation:

I soak in the benefits of peace and calm. My mind is relaxed and chill.

DAY 12: SEEING SYNCHRONICITIES

To be realistic, you have to believe in miracles.

— DAVID BEN-GURION

A *synchronicity* is when two things happen at (or near) the same point in time, in a way that is very unlikely, and possibly meaningful. For instance, thinking of some random, old song you haven't heard in years, and then that song plays on the radio. Freaky, right?

Skeptics argue that, with so much going on in the world, it's inevitable that chance events will occasionally line up, just as you'll eventually get ten heads in a row if you flip a coin enough times. Others suggest the more provocative idea that synchronicities are not mere coincidence, but that they have meaning, like a sign.

I understand the skeptics' point, but I also find the other possibility to be very exciting. And sometimes, extreme synchronicities can be *so effin' bizarre*, that even a stone-cold skeptic just has to shrug and say, "I got nothin'..."

I experience mini-synchronicities every couple of days. Maybe they are coincidences. And then, maybe once a month, I'll experience a *big one*. A doozy. Something that, if it's random chance, then the odds seem vanishingly small. Like, virtually impossible.

Are these meaningful? Signs from the universe?

I'd like to think so. And even if they're not, I think they still have value. They force me to pause and pay attention. They snap me out of my semi-automated day of doing routine things like working, checking email, cooking, exercising, etc.

Synchronicities shift your focus. They *feel* like little bits of magic being sprinkled into your life. And the occasional big synchronicities feel like *big magic*.

Don't let these magical moments go to waste!

Being aware of synchronicities is a cool, spine-tingling part of living a magical life. So compelling, it's a fun way to see the world, and sometimes the synchronicities make my jaw drop. As Elizabeth Lloyd Mayer writes in *Extraordinary Knowing*,

"Once we open the door to mind-matter anomalies, who knows what the rules are?... Can minds touch each other in ways that transcend mind and space as we understand them?"

It's a fascinating way to walk through life, being open and always asking, *What if?* At some point, you ask yourself where are all of these unbelievable experiences coming from, and you're deeply touched by how often things seem to line up, just for you. Sometimes things unfold so flawlessly, they line up so perfectly, that the rational mind is stunned into silence as your heart expands with awe.

Greg and I get a kick out of synchronicities. Here is one that happened recently: I sent Greg a text message telling him I wanted to discuss creating a *Coffee Self-Talk* coloring book for adults. A few hours later, I went to wake him up (he works late into the night). I crawled into bed and snuggled up next to him. We started chatting about business stuff, having one of our mini-biz meetings in bed. After reviewing a few things, I brought up the coloring book, and told him I thought it would make a great addition to the Coffee Self-Talk experience.

We had a brief conversation about it, and he loved the idea, so we put it on the list of things to research. Then, while we were still lying there, he reached for his phone to check the Coffee Self-Talk Facebook group.

And what do you think he saw?

The very first picture that appeared in the group was posted by a woman doing her Coffee Self-Talk *and coloring in a coloring book!* We laughed, and our eyes shot wide open. *"Holy shit!"*

That's a synchronicity. A little sparkle of magic. This is actually one of the mini-synchronicities. The big ones are a million times freakier!

Was this a sign from the universe?

Well, it certainly was a confirmation of sorts. Proof that at least some people would enjoy coloring while doing their daily Coffee Self-Talk. I like to think of it as a green light from a consciousness greater than mine, a meaningful wink from the universe. I mean, even if it's not, I think it's useful to *behave as if* it is meaningful. No sign from the universe is going to make me do something I don't want to do, but if it gives me a little nudge, or boost, or confidence, or motivation in the direction I was already considering? That's a wonderful thing!

We all experience these neat little glitches in the matrix from time to time, and I've come to treat them with awe and respect. They inject fun into the day and boost my confidence with a sense of playfulness.

Dr. Mark Hyman, in his article, *Coincidence or Synchronicity*, defines a synchronicity as:

> *"... a meaningful coincidence—an event on the outside that speaks to something on the inside—as opposed to just a random occurrence. If it means something to us, it automatically becomes something deeper."*

Synchronicities come in all different ways, shapes, and sizes. Once you start looking for them, you might start seeing them everywhere. All synchronicities are deeply touching to me, and ever fascinating. They can come from the most unexpected places and serve as a reminder to keep thinking and feeling your way to your magical life.

. . .

You are magical.

Today's affirmation:

I am a shimmering, glorious being. Synchronicities glitter all around me.

DAY 13: JUST ONE GOAL

"Success will be within your reach only when you start reaching for it."

— STEPHEN RICHARDS

Today, you're going to think about one goal that you have. Just one.

Did you know that just *thinking* about goals can make you happy? Literally. When you think about goals, motivation, and rewards, your body secretes dopamine, a feel-good neurotransmitter in your brain. In other words, when you imagine or expect a reward, like you would receive if you attained a goal, your brain secretes a happy chemical inside you from the expectation, and you feel good.

Why does your brain do this? Because it keeps you moving toward your goal, motivating you to take another step when you see a way to meet your needs. So when you constantly keep your goals and dreams front and center in your mind, it literally *feels good* because your body responds in support by triggering happy chemicals. Cool, huh?

The goal you choose to focus on for today's exercise could be anything from losing weight, to getting healthier, to getting better sleep, to getting a new job, to finding the love of your life, to manifesting a million dollars. Or it could be something small, like repotting a plant, or organizing your spice rack. Whatever it is, pick just one goal that you have.

You're going to close your eyes, and you're going to picture this goal. For example, if the goal is to travel, then you could picture in your mind a place you would like to take a trip. If your goal is to find the most amazing love of your life, then you might picture a romantic scene with you and your future partner, perhaps having a nice dinner, or snuggling in front of the fireplace.

If your goal is for health, or weight loss, or strength gains, then perhaps your mental picture is of your leaner body, or your healthier body, or bigger biceps, or maybe striking a pose in a bikini.

The idea is to create a picture that resonates with you and excites you. Adding color and detail to the picture will help make it more real in your brain. Even better, add sound, motion, and other sensory input.

Once you have your picture, you're going concentrate on it for the next few minutes, and you're going to feel amazing, high energy emotions while you think about this new you, or this new thing you want.

Imagine the possibilities!

Imagine what it would be like to have this thing you want, or to be this person you want to be, and *how awesome it would feel*. How would you stand? How would you walk? How phenomenal would your life be with this accomplishment or transformation?

You might not know exactly how it would feel, but that's ok, just accept that it'd simply feel amazing. If you need more help tapping into elevated feelings while you're focusing on your goal, you can just tap into feelings of gratitude, or awe, or love. I once did this exercise, and I thought about how much I loved my dog, and how great he was, and how much I enjoyed curling up with him. This prompted lovely feelings to course through my veins, while I then turned my focus to the goal I wanted to pursue.

With practice, or as more things manifest in your life, you will learn to tap into elevated emotions quickly and easily.

Your Turn to Play!

Once you've decided on a goal, set a timer for two minutes, and do the exercise I outlined above. Close your eyes, and go through the process of feeling the elevated emotions while you think about your goal.

When the timer is up, write down your goal, and describe

the picture you imagined in your head. Include as much detail as possible. As you recall the memory and write about it, your brain will continue filling in gaps, making the image more vivid.

Next, write down two actions you can take within the next 24 *hours* to make progress toward that goal. Your actions can be any number of things. Here are some examples:

Suppose you had a goal to earn $1 million. The two actions you write down can be what I call either *practical* or *magical*. "Practical" actions are those that any no-nonsense realist would agree could help you reach your goal. For example, to research alternative ways to make money.

"Magical" actions are those that help get your heart, spirit, and soul in the right state for realizing the goal. For example, to meditate for five minutes every day on this goal. And, of course, Coffee Self-Talk!

Practical actions might include reading a book about doing the thing you want to do. All you'd need to write on your list is: *read book*. Or maybe it's joining an online group of other people doing the same thing, in which case, you'd write, *join group*.

In other words, simple steps. Just to get things moving.

Magical actions might include loving yourself more, or working on feeling worthy, because feeling worthy is foundational to manifesting your dreams.

Better yet, choose one practical and one magical action.

For example, getting more sleep (magical, because it puts you in a better mental space) and reading the book (practical). Note how they work together here... when you're more rested, you'll have the clarity of mind and physical energy to read a book on the topic that'll help you move toward your goal.

And don't overlook the small goals; they are just as important as big ones. Accomplishing a small goal, like organizing your spices, builds momentum. Imagine the ease of making recipes with your spices (or kitchen) organized. Imagine buying spices you've never tried before. Imagine all the new recipes! Heck, maybe this one, small goal would set you in motion on a whole new trajectory, leading to a goal of writing a cookbook, or attending culinary school. You never know where things will lead!

You are inspiring!

~

Today's affirmation:

I love setting goals, and each step of progress toward my goals feels so good!

DAY 14: 10-SECOND PIXIE
DUST OF LOVE

"Happiness is a perfume you cannot pour on others without getting some on yourself."

— RALPH WALDO EMERSON

Today is an extra fun day because you get to focus your attention on your loved ones and the community. Even strangers!

Whaaat?

Sshhh! It's a secret!

It's profound. For both you and the person on the receiving end. And it's fun. I feel like a little magical fairy, going around sprinkling golden pixie dust of love on people.

Pixie Dust of Love Opportunity #1

Here's how you can join this juicy, happy lovefest. Throughout the day, when someone pops into your mind, no matter who it is, friend or foe, spend ten seconds wishing them love and happiness. Repeat for ten seconds,

I wish you love and happiness.

Say this no matter who it is!

If you find yourself having a hard time feeling love toward someone you think is not a nice person, well, then they need extra. After all, what makes people mean? That person probably doesn't have a lot of love in their life, and probably wouldn't be such a mean bean if they loved themselves. Here's the funny thing though... after sending some love their way, you'll feel better as a result. It's counterintuitive, but when you extend love to someone you don't like, it releases something negative from you. A darkness, or a weight, that you didn't know you've been carrying. And when it's no longer there, you're lighter. Freed from it. Happier. Try it yourself and see!

Pixie Dust of Love Opportunity #2

I first read about this idea years ago in Tim Ferriss' *Tools of Titans*, and I've been doing it ever since. When first meeting someone (or leaving someone, like leaving a lunch, or a meeting, or your friend's house), think to yourself about the person or people you were just with, *"I wish you love and happiness."* Repeat it for ten seconds for each person. You'll be amazed at how good it makes you feel.

Even more profound, repeat this for ten seconds whenever you're tempted to judge someone. Or again, when spending time with people that, let's just say, you'd rather not be stranded with on a desert island. Repeat it for ten seconds, sending them the love and happiness. *"I wish you love and happiness."*

Whoa... magic happens. Don't be surprised if you find yourself booking a cruise with them in the future! :)

Your Turn to Play!

Write *"Pixie Dust of Love!"* on several sticky notes. Then get your phone (or to-do list/calendar/notebook/etc.) and add it on there, too.

Whenever you see your stickies or reminders, stop, take a moment, and repeat one of the Pixie Dust exercises above.

You are pure love!

~

Today's affirmation:

I love spreading my love all over the world. It makes me feel wonderful and alive.

DAY 15: YOUR "I AM WORTHY" FOUNDATION

"You'll learn, as you get older, that rules are made to be broken. Be bold enough to live life on your terms, and never, ever apologize for it. Go against the grain, refuse to conform, take the road less traveled instead of the well-beaten path. Laugh in the face of adversity, and leap before you look. Dance as though EVERYBODY is watching. March to the beat of your own drummer. And stubbornly refuse to fit in."

— MANDY HALE, *THE SINGLE WOMAN: LIFE, LOVE, AND A DASH OF SASS*

Everything wonderful in life comes from a foundation inside you that knows *you are worthy*. If you want vibrant health, or to lose weight, or to bound out of bed with energy, you first need to feel worthy. When you want to make a lot of money, get a new job, or buy a new house, it'll all happen more easily when your dreams, goals, and plans are built upon a foundation inside you that knows *you are worthy*. The same applies when you are looking for the love of your life, or seeking to build a happy life with your partner. You will find your greatest romance when you attract from a foundation inside you that knows *you are worthy*.

Worthiness is the core. Worthiness is where self-love is hatched. Worthiness is security, and empowerment, and elevated emotions, and wholeness. *Knowing* you are worthy of everything you want is the foundation for *getting* everything you want. You become unshakable. You become bulletproof, metaphorically speaking.

I write romance novels under the pen name Brisa Starr. When I write my novels, I plan out my characters' arcs and journeys. That is, how they will grow and change by the end of the book. They all start out with problems or issues to work through as they progress toward their goals. By the time I started writing my fourth novel, a realization hit me: No matter what the character's journey is, their triumph came about only when the character realized they were worthy. Huh. Makes sense.

As I wrote more books, the same pattern kept repeating. At one point, I chuckled to myself, thinking people might stop reading my novels because all the characters just realize that they're worthy in the end.

But there is no other way.

We're all the main character in the novel of our lives. And our ability to progress all comes down to having a strong sense of self-worth.

Today, you're going to do some firing and wiring in your

brain that's dedicated specifically to worthiness. You'll do this with a simple and powerful affirmation:

I am worthy.

It's like a shot of espresso—small but mighty. It doesn't matter what happened in your past, or anything that you've done in your life, or last week, or yesterday. You are worthy of love and happiness. Period. Got that?

I promise that when you go through your day feeling worthy of everything you want, whether it's more love, or more beauty, or more free time, or more sales, or more happiness in your life, then it will happen, not only *when* you feel worthy, but *because* you feel worthy. The worthiness is *what makes it happen.*

Your Turn to Play!

Write "*I Am Worthy!*" on six sticky notes and place them where you'll see them throughout the day. Then add the sentence to your phone (or to-do list/calendar/notebook/etc.). The point is having this in multiple places to remind you. My favorite spots are my bathroom mirror, nightstand, refrigerator, car dashboard, my desk, and the door leading out to the garage.

Every time you see one of these reminders, stop and take a breath, and say (or think) the words, *I Am Worthy,* and really feel the epic stirring in your soul that comes with *truly* feeling worthy.

At first, you might not be used to this feeling, and that's ok. You might even cry as something releases inside you, knowing this is truth, and that it's been a long time since you've loved yourself like this.

Or you might have a resistant mindset that wants to say, "*Sorry, but I'm not worthy.*" It doesn't matter... **Do it anyway! Say the words!** You can just pretend, or imagine what it would be like to feel worthy. Even if you have doubts, just keep doing it. And the more you imagine this worthiness, the more you fire and wire this incredibleness in your brain, and eventually it will become natural to you.

Because... and I really, truly mean this...

You ARE worthy.

∽

Today's affirmation:

I am worthy of living my most magical, legendary life.

DAY 16: AN ABUNDANCE OF TIME

"What is a Wanderess? Bound by no boundaries, contained by no countries, tamed by no time, she is the force of nature's course."

— ROMAN PAYNE

Why is everyone always in a hurry?

I used to be. I was always cracking the whip on myself. *"I have to write 10,000 words today. I have to!"* Always cracking the whip on my daughter. *"Get your shoes on! We'll be late!"* Always on my husband, too. *"Did you finish the editing? The book cover? Tick tick tick!"*

Push push push!

You'd think I was giving birth. Every. Damn. Day.

Imagine the relief I felt when I discovered that I actually have an abundance of time. To do everything I want.

What?

How did I suddenly get an abundance of time? Did I hire a housekeeper? Did I hire a CPA? Did I outsource raising my daughter?

Nope. None of that.

What I did was, I started saying in my morning Coffee Self-Talk:

I have an abundance of time.

Yeah, that was it.

And then, something magical happened. When you tell your brain things like that, it rewires things and somehow just makes it true. I immediately started feeling lighter and more open. Wouldn't you, too, if you had an abundance of time?

After I added this simple line to my self-talk, whenever I thought about deadlines, I now started saying things like,

I have an abundance of time to write my book. I have an abundance of time to do whatever needs to be done. I have an abundance of time to get through all the items on my to-do list.

Something just *clicks* when you say liberating words like these. It frees up energy, your mind relaxes, and somehow, you're able to get done what you need to get done, but without a timeline. It's strange. Maybe a mindset of abundant time means deadlines *don't exist like they used to*. Or maybe having a relaxed attitude, and less tension, means being able to get more done because you're more efficient. It's hard to do things when you're under pressure.

I suspect that what's really going on here, or at least in part, is that when I think I have plenty of time, I feel happier and relaxed, and then, somehow, whatever needs to get done, just gets done. Kind of on its own. I just do it, without needing to crack the whip on myself. Sometimes, trying too hard works against you. Too much *try, try, try*, which starts triggering those nasty survival emotions. They help you when you need speed or strength—like in battle—but they sure as hell don't help you write five thousand words faster. Or better.

There's nothing magical about survival emotions. They don't belong in your magical life.

Benjamin Hoff's book, *The Tao of Pooh*, teaches the idea of *wu wei*. It's the notion that you live your life through *effortless doing*, that is, without struggle or antagonism. It's a philosophy of relaxing the death grip that time has on most people. Or that, when you try too hard at anything— racing around, frantically—it actually doesn't work. Life doesn't work. The author writes,

> "*When you try too hard, it doesn't work. Try grabbing something quickly and precisely with a tensed arm; then relax and try it again. Try doing something with a tense*

mind. The surest way to become tense, awkward, and confused is to develop a mind that tries too hard."

That's what happens when you rush. When you feel like you don't have time for things. You get tense, and it slams your mind shut, like a garage door with a broken spring. But by continuously telling yourself that you have an abundance of time, it relaxes you. It loosens your grip, so you actually get things done.

And for anything you don't finish, you're so chill and happy... *that you just don't care! Ha!*

Don't worry if it didn't get done today. There's always tomorrow.

Your Turn to Play!

Write *"I have an abundance of time"* on a sticky note, and place it where you'll see it when you do most of your work, such as at your desk.

Every time you see your note today, take a moment to relax, and allow yourself a deep breath. You don't need to rush. Why? Because you're a *kool kitty kat.* You have an abundance of time to get where you need to go, to do what you need to do, *and to be who you want to be.*

You are relaxed, calm, and effective.

∼

Today's affirmation:

I have an abundance of time to do everything I want to do. My life is magic.

DAY 17: HOW TO GET RID OF FEAR

"Fear is the path to the dark side. Fear leads to anger... anger leads to hate... hate leads to suffering."

— YODA

Fear.

Do you let it rule your life?

Do you make any decisions based on fear? For example, do you avoid eating certain foods because you're afraid of getting heart disease? Do you use certain beauty products or supplements out of fear? (I'm raising a hand here on this one. Fear of aging and wrinkles.)

Are you afraid to speak up about your needs at home with your spouse? Or even to your kids, because you're afraid they might not see you as supermom or superdad anymore? Or maybe you're just generally afraid to let your needs be known?

Are you afraid to speak up at work and let your boss know you're worthy of more money or more responsibility, or that you have an amazing idea? Is that you?

Have you ever failed to follow your dreams because you were afraid you might fail? Or failed to ask someone out on a date for fear of rejection?

If you answered yes to any of these, or if you thought of your own example where fear ruled the day, don't feel bad, you're not alone.

Fear: The Sneaky, Sly Fox

Fear is a sneaky little bastard. It's a sly fox... making you feel you have to over-protect yourself for fear of... well, all kinds of things: pain, physical injury, disease, emotional harm, failure, rejection, humiliation, aging... death. Fear is always there, riding shotgun, like a know-it-all, reminding you of what might go wrong. *What if you lose your job? What if it doesn't work? What if you get sick?*

Basically? Fear sucks.

It sucks not only because it makes you feel like crap, but also because it makes you less effective. It reduces blood flow to the brain. It prevents you from taking smart risks. It kills your creativity. It prevents you from finding solutions to challenges, like a dog who can't smell to find his buried bone. It diminishes your high vibe energy by switching your brain into survival mode. Fear even weakens your immune system. Over time, fear (in the form of stress and anxiety) will actually hasten death. How's that for protecting you from harm?

But I have great news. I'm going to tell you how to kick fear's butt. It's time to free yourself from the shackles of fear.

Take Time for Tea with Fear

What?

Hear me out. The first thing you must do is recognize that fear is only trying to protect you. It wants to help, which is kinda sweet. It masquerades as your BFF. Fear actually means well. But fear doesn't realize it's not helping you 99% of the time! Our brains' fear mechanism got dialed in during a time when saber-tooth tigers occasionally ate humans, and when getting banished from one's clan meant certain death. Look around... not a saber-tooth tiger in sight!

So why the heck is public speaking so scary?

Or asking for a raise?

They shouldn't be scary. Even if things go badly, they can't actually hurt you.

Unfortunately, feeling the emotion of fear in these "false alarm" instances actually *does* harm you. Physically, emotionally, and spiritually. It disconnects you from people, creativity, healing, *and solutions to your problems.*

So, we don't want or need most of the fear in our lives.

The exception is actual physical threats. If you're out camping in the Arctic, and you're being chased by a polar bear... by all means, be scared. That's legit.

The realization that fear is trying to help us (so cute), and that we usually don't require its assistance (so powerful), puts *you* back in the driver's seat. So, the next time you feel a little fear slithering up your spine, think about how it's only trying to help you, *and that you don't need it*. Next, kindly invite it in for a cup of tea, where you'll thank it for trying to help and letting it know it's not helping.

You might want to ask your fear a few questions.

- *Where did you come from?*
- *Do you ever help me? Have you ever hurt me?*
- *Have you ever prevented me from doing anything that, in hindsight, I wish I had done?*
- *If I ignored you, what's the worst that could happen? Could I handle that?*

And then the final step...

When you're done asking fear your questions, just let it go. All tea guests must eventually leave, and now it's *fear's* time to say goodbye.

If you like, say the following mantra out loud:

"I release all fears. Thanks for stopping by, fear, but I got this. I'm surrounded by love, and all is fine. I'm going to figure it out. Meanwhile, I'm going to just love right now. I release all fears. Right now. Goodbye."

After using this mantra a few times, you may wish to use the short version:

"I release all fears. Goodbye."

And one more tiny thing, for extra credit. This next part is a little corny, but it works, so just do it. After you say the mantra above, I want you to say, *"POOF!"* Adding funny little sound effects—and even a hand gesture—makes it more effective because your brain pays more attention. Trust me on this.

If you haven't already done the exercise above, now is the time to think of one of your fears, especially any fear that you feel unreasonably dominates your life. And then follow the steps above: Ask it for tea, ask it the questions, and then release it.

Or go one step further... literally make yourself a cup of tea, pour a second cup for fear, and then do the exercise. It's profound, and it will be an experience you'll remember so vividly that, if fear ever comes knocking on your door in the future, you'll remember your little tea party and chuckle.

You are fearless!

～

Today's affirmation:

I am brave, courageous, and bold. Watch me go!

DAY 18: GRABBING FOR GRATITUDE

"I don't think there are any limits to how excellent we could make life seem."

— JONATHAN SAFRAN FOER

Gratitude... such a lovely, lovely thing. It's powerful, uplifting, and it elevates your feelings of wholeness and love. It's a tested, tried-and-true way to boost happiness, because your appreciation of anything, in any moment, is always an easy way to turn your frown upside-down.

Gratitude is a simple way to change your thoughts to positive in an instant, and *that* gets you back on track to living your magical life. It rewires your brain, making it easier for you to see the good in any situation.

Dave Asprey, biohacker extraordinaire and inventor of Bulletproof Coffee™, writes,

*"Study after study shows that simple gratitude exercises...
can make you happier, more positive, and more emotionally
open after just two weeks. The benefits last, too, which leads
to an overall increase in well-being, making you stronger
and more resilient to stress."*

When I choose to experience gratitude, I often form a
picture in my mind of something I'm happy about, which
conjures a wave of gratitude that washes through me. I
have some go-to imagery, like sunshine. For me, sunshine,
even imagining it, makes me smile. It's bright, shiny,
warm, and luminous... all things I love. It reminds me of
summer, vacations, sun tans, and palm trees.

Another example, for me, is being grateful for things in
life that are easy to take for granted. Like technology,
search engines, and Wikipedia. These make research and
writing so much faster. I give thanks for being able to
write books in weeks instead of months because of them.

I'm grateful for coffee! Love it, love it, love it! I'm grateful
for libraries! I'm grateful for meditation. I'm grateful that I
have the power to feel happy at any moment. I'm grateful
for gratitude itself.

I'm even grateful for challenges. One thing I've learned,
time and again, is how something that first appears to be a
problem often turns out to be a guiding force for change,
propelling me forward, closer to my dreams. Or sometimes in a new direction completely. Every time this
happens, I'm in awe, and it makes me smile. It makes me

never want to resist "problems" again, and I'm grateful for this, too.

Today, you'll make a game of *Grabbing for Gratitude*. If you feel negative energy coming on, if something irks you, then grab for gratitude by shifting your thoughts to appreciation, which short-circuits the irk. This doesn't necessarily remove the problem, but it'll help diffuse the irksome situation and put you into a better mindset for solving the problem. And it'll get you back to living a magical life faster.

Your Turn to Play!

Think about two or three things that make you happy. They can be super simple things, like coffee or sunshine, but make them something you really, really love. These will be your go-to *objects of gratitude*.

Then, get four to six sticky notes and your phone (or to-do list/calendar/notebook/etc.). Write down your objects of gratitude. For example, I wrote down *sunshine*. And, of course, I use glitter pens and draw a little sunshine with a smile face on it and rays of love beaming out of it.

Place your gratitude stickies someplace where you'll see them occasionally. Seeing them will remind you of feeling gratitude, making you smile. When you do, close your eyes for a moment and really let the feeling soak in, deep inside. And it'll help you remember to grab for this gratitude object the next time you need it!

· · ·

You are inspiring.

Today's affirmation:

Gratitude flows like liquid gold in my veins. I appreciate things everywhere I look. Thank you. Thank you.

DAY 19: THE "I LOVE" GAME

"A thing of beauty is a joy forever."

— JOHN KEATS

Are you ready to have one of your best days ever? I'm teaching you how to play the game, "I Love."

Here's how you play:

You're going to spend the day constantly thinking about the things you love.

It's easy and fun!

Go get ten pieces of paper right now. They can be sticky notes or scrap paper with tape. On each of the ten pieces of paper, write:

I love _____.

And then fill in the blank with something you love. It can

be anything—tangible or abstract. Don't repeat any; make all ten of them something different that you love.

Here are some things I've written on my notes:

- I love coffee.
- I love oranges.
- I love steak.
- I love the sunshine.
- I love my toes.
- I love my bed.
- I love this chair.
- I love my laptop.
- I love my mom.
- I love my husband.
- I love trees.
- I love birds.
- I love the smell of vanilla.
- I love my daughter.
- I love fly swatters.
- I love blue sky.
- I love smooth pavement.
- I love stretching.
- I love swimming.
- I love boots when it's cold out.
- I love air-conditioning.
- I love my legs.

Just thinking of your ten items is enough to make this exercise worthwhile! It changes your focus and automatically helps boost your mood. It's pure gratitude!

But wait, there's more.

Now, take your notes and put them in random places around your home.

- I have one in the kitchen by the sink because I spend time there.
- I have one by my glass of water where I take my vitamins.
- I have one by my coffee station. Of course.
- I have one on the hallway mirror.
- I have one on my yoga mat.
- I have one on the table and my laptop covers it, so when I pick up my laptop and move it, I see it. Sneaky, huh?
- I have one on the door, so I see it when I leave the house.

The goal is not to only think about things you love—which happens when your write the notes—but also, for the notes to serve as reminders. You want the "I love _____" dialog running in your brain, repeatedly and somewhat randomly, for the entire day. No need to close your eyes, or breathe weird, or meditate on it. You don't even need to pull elevated emotions into the mix. Just think of something you love, and that will automatically trigger good feelings.

This fills your day with love and appreciation, but in a playful, light-hearted way.

And doing it with ten "I love" items starts to build this as a habit. After you've done this exercise a few times, you'll notice that you start thinking "I love _____" more often, about all kinds of things that you may have liked before, but you never stopped to appreciate just how much you loved them. Like scones!

And what a great habit. Simple, yes, and guaranteed to boost your mood.

Here is the next important step. At the end of the day, go around the house, pick up your notes, and put them in a zip-top bag, tucked away in your desk drawer or calendar for another day.

Saving these isn't meant to prevent you from creating ten new *I Love* items next time—I mean, thinking them up is half the fun. Rather, when you come across your old notes in the future, you'll get a little treat, a surge of pleasure, seeing and remembering what you wrote down last time.

Make the *I Love* game a purposeful activity that you repeat every few weeks or so.

You see things you love everywhere!

$\sim$

Today's affirmation:

I am kind and generous. I'm juicy, curious, and I love smiling.

DAY 20: RELAX THE DEATH GRIP

"Letting go gives us freedom, and freedom is the only condition for happiness. If, in our heart, we still cling to anything—anger, anxiety, or possessions—we cannot be free."

— THICH NHAT HANH

Living a magical life means relaxing the death grip of logic. I love this rule... *"relaxing the death grip of logic."*

Ahhhh, how great that feels.

You know what I mean? Just accepting that you don't have to know everything. You don't have to figure it all out. Certainly not today. You don't have to have thoughts of *"but how will my dreams manifest?"*

Sometimes, we force logic into every step of manifesting, which is a mistake. Logic and planning have their place, but the moment you feel yourself thinking the same thing over and over, you're in a rut. You need to step away from it. All too often, we ignore our intuition. Too much logic creates too many opportunities for doubt! And doubt does *not* attract our dreams and goals. We want confidence, and joy, and exuberance.

You don't have to know every detail of how something will happen, or how your future life will unfold. In fact, part of what makes your Coffee Self-Talk a tool for creating your magical life *is this* freedom, this surrendering to the unknown, this not knowing every little thing. You are free to tune into your intuition, your tastes, your feelings... and then kick back and see what the universe dishes up!

You hereby officially have permission to turn off your analytical brain today and go on a magical carpet ride with your intuition.

Listen to what it tells you!

I first came across the line, *"relaxing the death grip of logic"* in a book about Taoism by Derek Lin. It hit me so hard, it was like the sky split open and glittery stars came pouring out. It felt so good to do that... *relax the death grip of logic.*

Yeah!

You see, I had been a chronic over-thinker. About every-thing. I'd catch myself thinking in circles, driving myself batty at times. I was an over-analyzer by nature, until I learned it was causing stress and illness in me. I *knew, knew, knew,* deep down inside, I was not destined to rely on logic and analysis so much. My intuition was begging to be let out—I could feel it fluttering like a hummingbird trapped inside my chest, but I always kept it hidden.

Then one day, I started listening to my intuition, for the hell of it. I smiled so much that day. I asked my intuition questions... *and it answered!* I let it out to play, and suddenly, I felt free. It was also fun, like living in a fairy-tale world, letting go of my constant logic, and instead making choices by gut feel.

Hunches and intuition are incredible allies in a magical life. And letting go of rational thinking can often lead to *elevated feelings of relief,* because you simply don't have to have it all figured out. It's ok to not have all the answers. Nobody does! And that's a weight off your shoulders.

Suppose you wanted to be a millionaire, but you're a hundred thousand dollars in debt. With that crushing debt looming overhead, most people wouldn't be able to think for five minutes about becoming a millionaire. The rational mind would yank the reigns and say, *"Yeah right, how's that gonna happen?"*

But the person who is able to relax that death grip of their mind, the one who lets go and thinks about being a millionaire, *feels* how amazing and fun it would be, and doesn't get bogged down in negative, survival emotions of over-analysis... well, *that person* is the one who is more likely to succeed, because her mind isn't restricted by the debt. She's still free to dream, and set goals, think big, make plans, and take action. Emotion and excitement are the fuel. She'll figure out the path along the way.

Cramming too much logic into how to actually manifest your goal can cloak your dreams in dreary shadows.

When we overanalyze, we can't be as creative, which means we can't see as many opportunities. It gets stressful. It's no longer any fun. It throws sand into the gears of your manifestation. Sometimes we have to turn off the logic and tune into our intuition for guidance, assurance, and answers. Sometimes we have to let go, relax the death grip of logic, and simply *wonder, wonder, wonder...*

What amazing things are in store that you've never even dreamed of because you couldn't make sense of it logically?

There's only one way to find out.

Your Turn to Play!

Write *"Intuition"* on six sticky notes. Then get your phone (or to-do list/calendar/notebook/etc.) and add it on there, too. Stick the notes someplace where you'll see them today.

When you see the stickies, remind yourself to let go of logic for the day, when it comes to your magical life and dreams. Quiet your mind, and allow yourself to tap into your inner feelings, subtle knowing, and intuition. Let your intuition loose to play inside you today, and marvel at the wonder of it. Follow it, and see where it leads you.

You are incredibly capable.

Today's affirmation:

I feel like I'm riding on a shimmery, silver, magic carpet ride through the stars and night sky. I am filled with wonder and awe.

DAY 21: THE ENJOYMENT
SNIFF TEST

"Happiness consists in frequent repetition of pleasure."

— ARTHUR SCHOPENHAUER

How often do you ask yourself before doing anything, *"Will I enjoy this?"*

What are things you *actually* enjoy doing? A walk in the forest? A vacation? An evening with friends or family? Curling up with a book and a cup of tea, or a glass of wine? Surfing social media? Watching the news? None of those? All of those?

Two years ago, I didn't make decisions based on my level of enjoyment. I'd just say yes out of habit. Or a sense of obligation. Or not wanting to tell somebody no. Or because I just thought "I should," like going to a cultural event that, honestly, I had no interest in whatsoever. Am I really a better person for going to a *cheese museum?*

I failed to run these decisions through any kind of filter. I'm not referring to mandatory tasks, like going to work, paying bills, or doing the dishes. But rather, the optional things. The non-essential things. Such as watching TV, or going to some social activity. I failed to first ask myself, *Will I enjoy this?*

My life is very different now.

Enter: The Enjoyment Sniff Test

Now, I put most things through what I call the *Enjoyment Sniff Test.* Whenever I'm about to do something, or plan something, I first ask myself, *will I enjoy this?*

It's that simple. That's the Enjoyment Sniff Test. Just like a lovable, slobbery golden retriever, sniffing at something new to determine its worth, I sniff at things to do the same. *Sniff, sniff, sniff!*

Why is this important?

Because, darn it, most of us aren't enjoying our lives nearly as much as we could!

Look at your daily flow, or your weekly calendar, or some of the social commitments you've agreed to. If you don't really enjoy doing these things, that's not living a magical life.

As simple (and obvious) as it sounds, just asking that one, simple Enjoyment Sniff Test question—"Will I enjoy this?"—and then making an informed decision about what to do, will enable you to have more enjoyment in your life.

More enjoyment means more happiness! And research shows happy people are more productive, more likable, more resilient, and healthier. *They even live longer.*

Not to mention, happiness is an elevated emotion, which we all know by now, is essential to attracting your magical dream life.

I've learned a lot by doing my Enjoyment Sniff Test. I realized just how much I had been doing things that I didn't really want to do. Once I started focusing on my enjoyment, my life improved. Everything became much more enjoyable. *Ha!...* go figure. It allowed me to zero in on my own life more. My real priorities. And, in a funny way, I got to know myself better by doing this.

Learning to Say No

If you've been doing things you don't really enjoy, for reasons that are not related to other people, that's good news. It means the only person you have to convince is you. And all that requires is that you apply the Enjoyment Sniff Test to everything you do for a couple of weeks. If you've been stuck in a rut, or making decisions on autopilot, the sniff test will quickly instill the habit of making decisions more mindfully.

And then there's other people...

If you are going through life doing things you don't enjoy

out of a sense of obligation, guilt, *feeling unworthy*, or just not wanting to say 'no' or disappoint others (that's a big one), then you need to recognize that there's a cost to behaving this way. It takes a toll on you. In your health. In your happiness. It can seed resentment in relationships. It can dim your sparkle, or worse. In the long term, it can lead to feelings of deep regret for not having taken better care of yourself. That's no way to live your life.

These bad outcomes are *totally avoidable*.

But you must learn how to say no.

If you've been saying yes to everyone for a long time, this will be an adjustment. For you and them. But they will adjust, and so will you.

The trick is simply to explain why you're saying no. No one who loves you wants you to suffer. When you say no, be kind, but be honest. For example: *"I really appreciate the invitation, but I'm really working on myself right now, and I need to spend some time on that. Maybe we could do it in a few weeks."*

To repeat, nobody who loves you and cares about you should take issue with this. Or if they do, they're being unreasonably selfish. And you really don't need unloving or selfish people in your life. And if you're stuck with them (such as family), then you don't owe them anything so much that it harms you.

Sticking to your guns on this requires two things:

1. You must acknowledge that *your priorities are important.*

If this is difficult for you, it's a worthiness issue, and you should focus your Coffee Self-Talk script on this topic until it's fixed, because all happiness and magical living ultimately stem from having self-worth.

2. You must have the courage to be honest with those who love you. They might not understand at first. It's ok to ease into this, if that will help. Baby steps are fine. It might help them adjust to you becoming less flexible, or less available. But just make sure to keep applying the Enjoyment Sniff Test, and to be mindful when making your decisions.

If you do these two things, and apply the sniff test to all of your non-essential behaviors, you'll very quickly come to see just how much more enjoyment you'll experience, putting you well on your way to living your most magical life!

You are spectacular!

~

Today's affirmation:

My life is magnificent because I make it so.

DAY 22: OPPOSITE HAND DAY

"I'm choosing happiness over suffering... I'm making space for the unknown future to fill up my life with yet-to-come surprises."

— ELIZABETH GILBERT, *EAT, PRAY, LOVE*

Ok, let's take a break from working directly on the thinking and emotional centers of our brain, and focus our attention today on motor functions. *Aaaand,* in doing so, sneak in the back door to our thinking and emotional self.

This is what you call a *cognitive hack.*

Let me explain... by switching things up—simple, daily physical things, like how you brush your teeth—from how we usually do them, we can temporarily turn off part of the brain's autopilot system. Doing so makes us more self-aware, because we're literally *un-automating* behaviors that have become automatic over years of practice. And when we're more self-aware, we're better able to control everything our brain does, like our thoughts and emotions.

We're going to turn off these automatic motor functions by using our non-dominant hand. For instance, if you normally brush your teeth with your right hand, today, you'll do it with your left. It will feel weird. That's good though. That's the whole point of the exercise.

Six Benefits to Using Your Non-Dominant Hand

Using your non-dominant hand can yield some useful benefits in your life.

1. Mindfulness

Using your opposite hand makes you mindful while you're doing it, until you become good at it. In fact, you might need to really concentrate when you first begin. But as you adjust to this new way of doing a few tasks, you may begin to develop "methodical mindfulness," which means you're building the habit of doing things more mindfully in general... even with your dominant hand. That's what we're going for here, developing the habit of doing simple tasks mindfully, rather than on autopilot.

Once you've become proficient using your non-dominant hand at some task, the new behavior will eventually become automatic. And then, switching back to your normal hand might seem a little weird at first. But you'll always switch back much faster than it took to learn using the new hand, because the old wiring is already there in your brain.

2. Practicing Letting Go

Another thing to consider is how it feels awkward to use your non-dominant hand. It might even feel a little out-of-control. This can frustrate some people, make them grind their teeth. But this is an excellent exercise in *letting go* because not always being in control, or rigid, or tight, helps you learn to let go of frustration and anxiety when things happen in life that are beyond your control, which is inevitable. The more controlling, Type-A your personality is, the more important it is to practice letting go. (Your teeth's enamel will thank you.)

By experiencing frustration while doing something with your non-dominant hand, and then breathing through it and letting the frustration go, you build up your *letting go muscle*, and that is a superpower. Besides, there's not much downside risk to brushing your teeth goofily for a few days. (Don't do this using power tools or sharp objects!)

3. Mindfulness + Self-Talk = Magic Brain Stuff

Returning to the first benefit, mindfulness, this switching-hands exercise is also a great time to say a line from your Coffee Self-Talk. That is, saying one of your affirmations repeatedly while you're using your non-dominant hand.

For example, while you're washing dishes with your opposite hand, you can repeat a beautiful mantra like, *"I love my life. I love my life. I love my life."* You're taking advantage of a time your mind is in a mindful mood and layering in positive affirmations at the same time. This imbues the self-talk with extra power, because your brain is paying extra attention to everything that's happening, and rewiring itself.

In contrast, if you say your self-talk while brushing your teeth (etc.) with the hand you usually use, it can still be easy for your mind to drift to random thoughts or thinking about things you need to do that day. But repeating your self-talk while brushing with your non-dominant hand keeps you extra focused, and slipping in some affirmations in the process is like extra credit. Try this out, and you'll see what I mean!

4. Comedy

Let's face it, awkward things are funny. Like if a dog tried to make pancakes. When you attempt new things with your non-dominant hand, it's funny. You might make mistakes, or spill something, but it's a practice in laughing at yourself, which is elevating your emotions. It's fun and goofy, so laughing is not only welcome, it's highly recommended. Even more fun is involving the whole family. Kids especially love this activity!

5. Posture

For certain activities, using your non-dominant hand can cause improvements in your posture. A physical therapist once told my husband, the best position for the body is *the next one*. Meaning, you should never stay in the same position too long. Making changes to your position and posture increases circulation and prevents stiffness from setting in.

One way to take advantage of this is by using your computer's mouse with your non-dominant hand. You'll feel how it changes circulation from moving and sitting in a way you rarely do. It also rests your dominant hand, and with something like using a mouse if you work all day at a computer, these brief breaks can help prevent repetitive strain injuries (RSIs) such as tendinitis and carpal tunnel syndrome. Clearly, this isn't the kind of exercise to do if you're on a deadline or doing precision work, but it's quite doable with less demanding tasks such as email, browsing the web, etc.

6. Confidence Boost

If you do any of these things repeatedly, then you will have a new skill, which will boost your confidence. It's also a lot of fun learning new skills.

It's helpful, especially as we age, to learn something new, as often as possible. Not only because it's good for brain health (which it is), but also because it reminds us that we're *still teachable*. I mentioned in the book, *Coffee Self-Talk*, how my father-in-law taught himself to shoot Olympic-level archery in his seventies. Imagine the confidence that would give anyone at his age, someone who might otherwise be intimidated to learn something new, like a software application or other technology.

Learning new stuff regularly keeps us sharp and makes us confident to always keep attempting new things.

Some Ideas to Try

I have a history of eating food too fast. Not being mindful, barely chewing, swallowing a whole mouthful at a time... like when you toss a steak to a big dog and *shlurp*... it's just gone. I don't know why, but it's been a habit since I was young. In fact, when I was a teenager, my parents would call me for dinner when they were already halfway through *their* dinner, because otherwise, I'd finish eating before they'd even put all the food on their plates.

To help change this habit, I tried putting down my fork between bites. That lasted about one meal. I tried counting chews, but that drove me bonkers.

And then, I tried eating with my non-dominant hand.

Wouldn't you know it? I slowed down, naturally. Hell, I had no choice, otherwise I'd have accidentally poked myself in the cheek with my fork. So when I started eating with my non-dominant hand, a kind of calm was forced on me, an attention to detail in the mechanics of eating. I actually enjoyed my food more! My digestion thanked me. And my mindfulness increased, as well as my time at the table with my family. And there were no more starving-dog *shlurp* noises!

Other Ideas for Using Your Non-dominant Hand

- Making your morning coffee!
- Texting
- Opening doors

- Turning on/off light switches
- Washing dishes... just switch the hands you use for holding the dish and sponge, etc. (You might not want to try this with your fine bone china teacup!
- Opening jars
- Eating
- Drinking
- Brushing or combing hair
- Pouring drinks (remember, laughing if you spill)
- Cooking and baking
- Playing ping pong
- Using a computer mouse

Whichever ones you try, just be sure to have fun!

You are creative!

~

Today's affirmation:

Learning new skills is fun. It adds energy and a splash of adventure to my life.

DAY 23: YOUR POWER, YOUR RESPONSIBILITY

"The trick is in what one emphasizes. We either make ourselves miserable, or we make ourselves happy. The amount of work is the same."

— CARLOS CASTANEDA

Batter Up!

Step up to the plate. You have the power. It's you. It's *all* you. Today, now, tomorrow, and ongoing. All you, baby.

Your power, your responsibility. This should excite you. Your magical life is *not* under the control of others. In fact, by not taking responsibility for your own thoughts and feelings, you leave your mind and heart—*and your whole future!*—open to the whims of others. *Gah!*

This is true, even if you come from a troubled past—lots of us do. Sadly, it's not even particularly rare or noteworthy. But some people manage to overcome their difficult pasts, while others don't. What sets some people free?

It's impossible to manifest powerfully when you've got a victim mentality. That low energy and those limited feelings are out of alignment with your dream life's high energy that you want to draw toward you. They're opposites that repel each other—like oil and water.

So when you're calling your bright future to you, it's important to do it from a place of fun and loving emotions, or ones of awe and gratitude, or excitement and adventure. Not from scarcity, anger, distrust, resentment, or feeling limited.

Not from fear.

There are many opportunities to choose elevated emotions throughout the day, and through your entire life. It's a choice. **You get to choose!** What one person sees as bad, another might not. *"One man's trash is another man's treasure."* It's about perspective, and what you can do about a situation, how you choose to respond. If something doesn't go your way, it's your job to choose—out of the hundreds of possible ways—how you respond.

It's *your* job.

I had been experimenting with this idea of getting better at dealing with adversity, when an opportunity to do so presented itself.

To the tune of $600 dollars lost. *Ouch.*

People go on *Judge Judy* for way less than that.

I had booked international air travel pre-COVID, but after COVID hit, and flights were getting cancelled left and right, we finally managed to get new tickets. But in the shuffle, the airlines had lost the records of the fees we'd paid for extra luggage and seat upgrades to avoid having our knees jammed into the seat in front of us for eight hours while crossing the Atlantic.

The ticketing service told us to take it up with the airlines, but the airlines were so swamped, none of them were answering their help lines. It was nerve-wracking, annoying, and frustrating as hell. My chest squeezed tight as I contemplated spending *another* $600 for the luggage and seat upgrades on the new tickets.

But in that moment, my curiosity made me pause. At that time, I was swimming in full-on transformation, drinking my own Kool-Aid, elevating my emotions for a better life. So I asked myself, *"Is there better way to handle this?"*

I realized, yes, there was. I imagined, if I were a millionaire, I might not care about getting the refund. My time might be more valuable than the hours it would take to fix the situation. The whole situation would have much less emotional impact—an annoyance perhaps, but not a gut punch.

Call me crazy, but I *instantly* felt better. It didn't change the fact that I might be out $600, but it didn't feel as ugly. My vibration lifted higher. And I realized, wow, I could do this in any situation.

Imagine the possibilities.

What would you attempt if you were emotionally bulletproof?

And then, because the universe is winky, that very same day, a freaky synchronicity occurred when an Instagram image appeared on my phone:

> *"You know you've mastered yourself when the circumstance has not changed, but the way you respond has."*

Wow.

Tears of joy and relief fell from my eyes. They're even wetting now, as I write this, because I get such goose bumps. I thought, *You're on the right track, girl.*

I managed to shrug off the $600, which allowed me to focus on the much more important business of wrapping things up before traveling, and living my happy life.

Funny thing is, two months later, it occurred to me that I should issue a chargeback with my credit card. I logged on to my bank to track down the details... *and there it was.* The $600 refund had come in just a few days earlier.

All that stress *for nothing.* Any additional time or energy spent dwelling on the subject would have been totally wasted. Worry and stress were unnecessary. Everything worked itself out.

It reminds me of the serenity prayer:

> *"Grant me the serenity to accept the things I cannot change, the courage to change the things I can, and the wisdom to know the difference."*

Your power to choose how you react is a superpower.

Nobody can ever take it away from you.

Two more quick examples:

1) Imagine two people catch a cold. One of them stresses about it, spending a few miserable days in bed, lamenting his bad luck. The other person shrugs, knows this happens sometimes, and says, *"Now, I can finally binge-watch Grey's Anatomy."*

Aside from enjoying *Grey's Anatomy*, the second person is actually more likely to recover faster due to being less stressed by the whole thing.

2) Imagine two people lose their jobs. One person gets scared, but the other person says, *"Looks like that door has closed. Time to open a new one. What fantastic opportunity is coming my way now?"*

I get emails all the time from readers who left their jobs (voluntarily or not), only to end up in *much* a better situation within a couple of weeks. The stories all share a common thread: When they left their job, even if they were scared, they saw it as an opportunity for positive change.

I could go on and on. The point is, you are in control of how you respond to life's events. And you can use these situations to practice improving your self-mastery with high-energy emotions. Those elevated emotions will draw your dreams closer to you faster.

You can even view these situations as an opportunity to

springboard onto an amazing new path of unknown life adventures!

You are brilliant!

~

Today's affirmation:

I am the conductor of my amazing life. I show up to it every day, shoulders back, grin on my face.

DAY 24: MIGHTY AFFIRMATION DAY

"Keep your best wishes, close to your heart, and watch what happens."

— Tony DeLiso

Today's exercise is simple, but it is powerful for helping you remember to tap into the elevated feelings you had earlier in the day when doing your Coffee Self-Talk.

"Repetition is the mother of skill."

— Tony Robbins

I first heard this quote by Tony Robbins in my twenties. It has stuck with me ever since. Repetition is important because the opportunity to master a any skill, technique, or mindset is greatly improved when you repeat it. That is why we have *Mighty Affirmation Day*.

Doing your Coffee Self-Talk ritual in the morning is amazing, when you're firing and wiring your new mindset, your new elevated emotions, and your new, brilliant, spectacular you. But later, a few times during the day, you can tap into one of your uplifting, rainbow-awesome affirmations, and drill that state of mind even deeper into your soul.

That's the secret to faster transformation. Carrying your self-talk beyond the morning ritual is how you make your dreams come true faster, and with more ease.

Your Turn to Play!

Select one affirmation from your Coffee Self-Talk script, and then write it on six sticky notes. If you haven't read Coffee Self-Talk, then select one of the affirmations in this Daily Reader (there's one at the end of each day), or feel free to write your own.

Next, get your phone (or to-do list/calendar/notebook/etc.) and add the affirmation there, too. Pick two places on your to-do list or calendar. You want this in multiple places to remind you.

Now put your sticky notes someplace where you'll see them during the day.

Each time you see your note, take a moment to read the words, out loud if possible. Really try to *feel* them, emotionally. Tap into that magic, the incredible energy of your vision. Think it, feel an elevated emotion, like love, or awe, or happiness while doing this, and draw your dreams to you faster.

You are full of power.

～

Today's affirmation:

My words are my power. My thoughts shine my light.

DAY 25: CHANGE YOUR NAME

"Ever since happiness heard your name, it has been running through the streets trying to find you."

— HAFEZ

Today, we've got a super fun game. It's a way to play with the universe and elevate your spirit for a split-second, like a jolt of happy electricity zipping through you.

Email Newsletters and Coffee Shops

When I sign up for email newsletters, when the form asks for my name, I always provide a made-up name that's fun, playful, uplifting, and powerful. Then, every time the email newsletter comes into my inbox, I see the fun name, and it's like someone else is calling me that name, too. Which, for a second, trips me up in the most fantastical way. It's like social proof of your awesomeness.

Wow! Someone besides me realizes how awesome I am!

Even once you snap back to reality and remember that you're the one who gave you the name, and it's just a computer somewhere repeating it, you'll still smile at the playfulness of it all. And it feels good, because it feels so right being referred to with super cool words!

Examples of names I've used:

- *Magic Beauty*
- *Money Maker*
- *Sparkle Twilight*
- *Happy Sexy Millionaire*
- *Awesome Kristen*
- *Clever Lady*

I also do this for things like tracking emails from the post office. If I have a package coming, and I have the tracking number, they offer to send email updates on the delivery progress and status. It's extra special receiving one of these, with my new name, from the U.S. government! I mean, that makes it *official*, right?

Pro tip: Don't try this with the IRS.

I love doing it at coffee shops, too. It's a triple wallop of fun. When they ask me my name to write on the cup, I get creative. I give them a name such as:

- Shooting Star
- Glitter Rainbow

- Love
- Happy Unicorn
- Magic

I get three sparks of happiness. The first comes when I tell the barista what to write on the cup. I always get a grin or a chuckle. I get a kick out of this, and it makes their job a little more fun, too. Plus, someone else is writing it, which means I get their buy-in! Social proof!

The second burst of fun comes when the barista calls my name, once my drink is ready. When it happens, it *really* feels like the universe is giving me a giant, cosmic thumbs-up.

As the barista calls my name out in front of everybody, a jolt of playful love zips through my body. Other customers often look up and chuckle, half amused, and half curious to see what kind of person goes by the name, *Shooting Star.*

The third tickle of joy comes each time I see my cup the entire time I'm drinking my delightful concoction. I turn the cup so I can see it, and it really does continue to amuse for the next half hour or so. But it's also doing something to my self-identity... I can actually feel the words imprinting on me. Like a name, or a title. It's not just a fun game, it really makes you see yourself in a different light.

The next time you order coffee (or phone in an order to Chipotle), or sign up for a newsletter online, give this a try!

. . .

You are fun!

Today's affirmation:

I radiate high-energy frequencies day and night, and they attract that which I desire into my dream life.

DAY 26: DOWN THE RAINBOW RABBIT HOLE

"For every minute you are angry, you lose sixty seconds of happiness."

— RALPH WALDO EMERSON

When something is disturbing you, or when something feels jagged inside and not smooth, ask yourself, *"What bothers me about this? And why?"*

Whether it's something you saw on social media, or something you heard at work, or something your dad or brother or sister said, ask yourself, "What bothers me about it?"

But don't stop there, go down the rainbow rabbit hole. Ask again, *"Well, and what bothers me about that?"* And on and on, like the four-year-old who keeps asking "why?" no matter what answer is given.

This is not the time to fix anything. You're just probing

your mind to see what answer comes up. You're not fighting the answers you get. There's no battle here. On the contrary, you're relaxing, observing. You're *releasing your awareness.* All you have to do is ponder *why* something bothers you, and keep going down the rainbow rabbit hole until you reach the bottom, and there's nothing left.

When you drill down to the bottom, you'll find that most of the things that bother you boil down to some sort of fear. Fear of rejection, fear of embarrassment, fear of illness, fear of failure, fear of success, fear of being alone, fear of dying.

So, let's now take that fear and objectify it. Fear is, after all, just *a thing.* So imagine your fear like an object. Something small that could fit in your hand, like a shiny, black cube. By objectifying your fear, you can disconnect from it emotionally and comprehend it objectively, like it's outside of you.

If you feel a fear, imagine that fear as the black cube, and pull it out of you. Notice how it fits nicely in the palm of your hand. Now, put the cubed fear that's in your hand, and hold it out in front of you at arm's length. Just look at it. It's not inside you. It's out... there.

The first time I did this, I realized I could say to the cube, "Oh, it's that fear thing."

It's a... thing.

It's not me.

In your best poker voice, you say, *"I see you fear, and I raise you a bucket full of love."*

When you look at fear this way, it helps you *let go of it,* so you can get back to your epic living. The fear can no longer bother you, unless you let it. Remember, a few moments ago, you were fine. Life was rolling along. Then the thing happened that bothered you, and it created this little fear object you're now holding in your hand. Well, since you were fine a moment ago, you can get right back there.

All you have to do is visualize placing that little fear object on a shelf, and walking away.

Goodbye, little fear object. Thanks for trying to protect me, but I'm good.

After doing this rainbow rabbit hole exercise a few times, you won't even need to do the visualization part. You'll just come to recognize that the thing that bothers you is motivated by some unnecessary fear, and you'll banish it. *BAM*, just like that. Gone. Back to living your lovely, glowing, magical life.

With this new, fear-banishing superpower, instead of getting distracted or bummed out by things that bother you, these situations wake you up! They remind you that *you're in charge!*

And even more, the experience doesn't leave an emotional scar in its wake. It's like drawing in the sand—it's there, and then it's gone. The idea is not that you'll never experience fear... you will. We all do. That's normal. It's that you have the ability to look at it differently, from an outside perspective, digging in a little to understand it and learn that it doesn't have a hold on you, and letting it go. Going down the rainbow rabbit hole and asking why something bothers you helps you separate yourself from it, and move on.

Enjoying this level of freedom means you understand that temporary shifts of energy are just that, temporary. When you feel pain, or when something bothers you, view it as fluid energy. You can open your hand and just let it go. It just drifts away, like steam coming off a hot drink.

Whatever issue—the root fear—that you reveal down in the rabbit hole can be healed. It's a moment to celebrate, because the hardest part is identifying the cause. Once you've done that, it only takes a moment to make a change from recognizing this energy pattern in you, to letting it go.

And if you should happen to experience the same fear again in the future, that's ok. You now recognize its face, and you can be that much quicker to show it the door before it brings your mood down. The more often this happens, when you keep letting go, over and over, a more elevated flow of energy inevitably takes its place. More peace, more love.

In this way, you process negative emotions faster, which means you can jump back into your amazing shiny, luminous life. The life you're destined to live. All. The. Time.

Your Turn to Play!

If you're in a great mood, and don't want to dredge up anything that bothers you, that's no problem. Keep this technique handy for the next time something comes up.

But if you're feeling adventurous or introspective, then think of something that's happened—maybe recently, maybe some time ago—that bothered you. Nothing major, the point isn't to dig up any traumas here. Baby steps... start with something small. Perhaps something that happened at work, or in traffic, that you've had a hard time letting go of.

Picture that event, and then go down the rainbow rabbit hole, as described above. Identify the root fear, then objectify it into a small object. You can even ask it questions, if you like!... It can't hurt you.

And when you're done examining it, just let it go.

You are equipped to handle anything!

∼

Today's affirmation:

My heart and mind are wondrous, and I'm grateful for my life.

DAY 27: ALWAYS SEE LOVE FIRST

"Just because you are happy does not mean the day is perfect. It means that you have looked beyond its imperfections."

— BOB MARLEY

Today, no matter what comes up, you're going to see *LOVE* first.

It's simple, but so powerful. A small, intentional act like this boosts your emotions, diffuses negativity, and gives you a needed pause. Love will always be the best way to lead, whether healing from illness, solving a problem, dealing with a difficult person, or pursuing a dream.

Love will always lead you out of darkness.

Mediation helps in a similar way. When you meditate regularly, and then you run up against stressful situations in your day-to-day life, you're able to handle those situations in a much better frame of mind. The meditation has trained you to notice your reaction and *pause*... before over-reacting, losing your shit, or saying something you'll later regret. This pause gives you clarity and prevents your emotions from making matters worse, and sometimes diffuses situations altogether, by making you calm, collected, and in a more resourceful mental state. This equanimity makes navigating the waters of life so much easier. It prevents a lot of arguments, and probably a lot of divorces, too.

It's the same idea with seeing love first.

When you train yourself to automatically *see, think, and feel* a cute little fluffy moment of love when dealing with people, situations, or things that might otherwise burn your feathers, a surprising number of these situations just sort of magically resolve themselves, or downgrade to something mild you can shrug off, or chuckle about.

A few years ago, we were housesitting all over Europe as a way to do long-term travel without paying for lodging. Housesitting is not widely known, and I thought, *Wow, this is such a great way to travel. I should share it on my blog.* But getting the best housesits (castles even!) can be competitive. It crossed our minds that sharing this best-kept secret with the world might increase the competition, making it harder for us to get great houses.

But that didn't feel right.

It felt selfish. Greedy. Oily in my stomach. At the time, I wasn't yet doing Coffee Self-Talk, and this was before my *dark-night-of-the-soul* transformation (which is described briefly in *Coffee Self-Talk*, and in detail on my blog). I was, however, already well into my journey of meditation and Taoism. So it didn't resonate with me to do things based on selfishness or greed.

In that moment, I just sort of flipped a switch. I suddenly felt love and compassion for all the people and families who would love the opportunity to travel doing housesits. I felt as though my life started shimmering like gold. What a different feeling! Same topic—blogging about housesitting—but now, I had a totally different energy toward it.

So I started blogging about it. I even wrote a book about it! More openness. More creativity. More opportunities.

Now, I always see love first. It's my default filter, the lens through which I view the world. And it's a more beautiful world this way!

Imagine you're in a meeting, and your coworker has an opinion that differs from yours. See love first, before anything else.

Do you have a child who hasn't done what you've asked them to do? See love first, and immediately notice how much more patient you become.

Do you have a loved one who is insecure and acting out? See love first, and compassion flows. Do you have a friend who is being uncool? See love first, and feel the soothing from that. Can you think of a politician who is, shall we say, *less than ideal?* See love first, and you'll sleep better at night.

How Do You See Love First?

It's easy. You simply think about love, like the feeling of love, hearts, and sweetness. Cotton candy, puppies and kittens, cooing baby-type sweetness. I don't mean that you actually think of cotton candy, though you can. I mean that this feeling of love you touch in this moment is light, airy, and soft. It's warm and cozy, like a blanket. The feeling is easy to feel if you focus on it, and incredibly powerful in its effect.

When you take a moment to focus on love, it'll create a pause, giving you a welcome moment to settle down, not get riled up, and to relax in the face of adversity. Of course, it'll also make you happier and feel better. It creates a more elevated emotional experience—or at least, it'll calm down any potentially negative boiling in your gut to a gentle simmer. That's an improvement!

You see love all around you.

∼

Today's affirmation:

I see love first, in all situations.

DAY 28: JOKES & LAUGHING

"Laughter is an instant vacation."

— Milton Berle

How true is that quote? I love it.

Yes, laughing is a vacation. And we could all use more laughing in our lives. I'm not sure there's ever enough! Even when my face and stomach ache from laughing, I still want more. Laughing till I cry, laughing till I snort, laughing is one of my favorite things to do.

Laughing is great for many things. Apart from it just being *fun*, laughing is also especially great for manifesting. Why? Because laughing *feeeeeels* good, and when your emotions are elevated and aligned with your intentions, that's when the sparkly magic happens.

We now know that when we're designing our dream life, there are two key elements to making it happen. The first is *thinking* the thought of what you want in life. The second is *feeling* elevated emotions to put out a positive vibe that somehow seems to magically draw toward you the dream life you've envisioned. And so, making sure you find time to laugh is a magnificent way not only to feel good in the moment, but also to start creating your magical future.

The immediate effects aren't just your imagination. Laughing causes your body to secrete endorphins, which legit makes you happy. It even switches on the expression of genes that help you heal.

So how can you have more laughter in your life?

Scientific American's article, *What's So Funny? The Science of Why We Laugh*, states that people think it's funny when expectations and reality contradict one another. When these contradictions are harmless, we laugh. "To wit: 'I was wondering why the Frisbee was getting bigger, and then it hit me.'" *Haha.*

Matthew M. Hurley, author of *Inside Jokes: Using Humor to Reverse-Engineer the Mind*, wrote on his website about these contradictions, "Humor is related to some kind of mistake. Every pun, joke, and comic incident seemed to contain a fool of some sort—the 'butt' of the joke." This observation led him to ask, "Why do we enjoy mistakes?" and to propose that it is not the mistakes per se that people enjoy. It is the "emotional reward for discovering, and thus undoing, mistakes in thought. We don't enjoy *making* the mistakes; we enjoy weeding them out."

In other words, humor is a reward we give ourselves for figuring something out.

So, things that make people laugh are contradictions, unexpected twists, bloopers, and jokes. You can also catch laughter from someone. This even works on yourself. Try this: Start with a forced laugh, and if you keep it up, you will soon laugh for real.

All the more reason to not take ourselves too seriously. Make mistakes, laugh at them, and learn.

Your Turn to Play!

Make a list of three things that make you laugh, and do them now, or plan them for later. Here are some ideas to get you started:

1. Watch a 30-minute comedy on television. My family cracks up with *Brooklyn Nine-Nine*, and my mom and I still laugh hysterically at old episodes of *I Love Lucy.* (*Candy Factory*, anyone? Or *Vitameatavegiman*?)

2. Make goofy faces at yourself in the mirror, and force laughter at yourself until it's real.

3. Look up jokes online. I'll go first:

Joke #1

What's the best thing about Switzerland?

I don't know, but the flag is a big plus.

— READER'S DIGEST

Joke #2

Why don't scientists trust atoms?

Because they make up everything.

— Reader's Digest

Joke #3

A man is struggling to find a parking space. "Lord," he prayed, "If you open a space for me, I swear to give up beer and go to church every Sunday."

Suddenly, the clouds part, and a beam of sunlight shines on an empty parking spot. The man says, "Never mind, I found one!"

— Unknown

You see humor everywhere!

⌇

Today's affirmation:

I love laughing, and it makes my heart sing.

DAY 29: IS YOUR CUP OVERFLOWING?

"A flower blossoms for its own joy."

— OSCAR WILDE

Have you got too much on your plate? Do you ever fill your cup with so much information on a subject, or things to do, that it's overflowing?

When I get going on a project, or start learning something new, I can get so excited about it that I'll have fifty tabs open on my laptop, multiple books ordered, and a dozen YouTube videos queued up to watch.

And it's all exciting, right? My energy is jazzed like I'm mainlining coffee. I get amped up because I'm learning something new and great!

But. When this happens, it's easy to overdo it. As you add more and more, pretty soon, your cup fills to the brim, and it overflows. Your brain can only hold so much at a time.

Sometimes, trying to manifest too hard can get like that. You get so excited, and you start doing so much to help make your dreams come true, faster, that you rush the process. You try, try, try! *Hurry up, dreams, I'm doing all the self-talk and the work, hurry! I want my new life... NOW!* (Cue Veruca Salt, the spoiled girl from Willy Wonka, yelling *"I want it now!"*)

Then, you crash and burn. You've overdone it. Your energy changes from relaxed openness to tight and closed. That's not the path for a magical life.

The whole process of living your most magical life is living a life filled with happy emotions. Feeling uplifted, shimmering with a glow. That means not rushing things or falling prey to survival emotions. It means not pressuring yourself. It means patience and being gentle and kind with your heart.

Patience and gentleness foster love and positive energy. And it's those emotions that will end up helping you make your dreams come true. Don't feel as though you must rush manifestation—any sense of urgency comes from survival emotions. Like scarcity, or fear of loss.

The list of possible actions you could take on any given day is infinite. Don't feel you have to do a hundred of them, or even ten, today. Or your cup might overflow. And that will dump your manifesting mojo right into the sewer. It's better to take on fewer items, and work through them with patience, thoughtfulness, grace, and style.

For people on a mission, this slowing down requires discipline. But if your cup has been overflowing, you'll be amazed at the difference. Your work will improve, and you might even avoid making costly mistakes.

In the James Bond novels, 007 would never set the bomb to detonate and then run away. He always walked. Why? To avoid tripping. Plus? It's just cooler. That's you. Not running through your day going crazy, but rather, walking like a badass superspy. *Kaboom!*

Your Turn to Play!

If you're working overtime at your job or on a personal project, and things are getting a little intense or overwhelming, then dial things down a notch. If there's not an actual, make-or-break deadline, then take a rest. Sometimes you just have to close the laptop, close the books, close your eyes, and take a soft breath. Take time to enjoy things and not run through life like your hair is on fire.

You are wonderful.

～

Today's affirmation:

My life is relaxed and calm. I breathe in and out with ease.

DAY 30: UNCONDITIONAL HAPPINESS

"When the first baby laughed for the first time, its laugh broke into a thousand pieces, and they all went skipping about, and that was the beginning of fairies."

— J.M. BARRIE, *PETER PAN*

I'd like to give you a permission slip. It gives you permission not to care what's happening outside your world, except when you want to. It gives you permission to focus 100% to keep working on anything you want, to expend all of your available energy pursuing your dreams.

There's a global crisis happening? You don't have to give it your energy. Something bad happened to someone else? You can offer loving thoughts, but you have the right to keep moving toward your dreams. Just because something has happened to someone else does *not* mean it needs to bring you down.

The idea—and this may sound radical—is to keep your emotions elevated through *everything*. When you do this, you're living in what's called *unconditional happiness*. And when you do it, you're putting a stake in the ground. You're taking a stand. You're making a point, and you're even serving as an example to others.

Here's how it works...

Whenever something unpleasant happens, simply state the following:

"My happiness is not based on _____."

One way to do this is to fill in the blank with the opposite of the bad thing. For instance, if you have a headache (or PMS, or a broken toe, etc.), you'd say:

"My happiness is not based on not having a headache."

Or if you had your heart set on buying a particular house, and someone else bought the house before you could put down an offer, rather than feeling sad, you'd say:

"My happiness is not based on living in that house."

And there you go. No problem. Now you can start looking for a different house with a clean slate, an open mind, and no regrets.

This simple, but powerful, statement is the embodiment

of you choosing to be happy during less-than-ideal circumstances.

It can apply to any situation. You simply decide when you'd like to apply it.

For instance, you may feel that it would be inappropriate to feel happy during certain times, such as a natural disaster or other tragedy, the death of a loved one, or while you're processing some other significant bad news. And that's ok. But keep in mind, an elevated emotional state makes you better equipped to respond to any situation, which can make you a resource to others in their time of need. Or to yourself, in your time of need... such as healing from injury or disease, or when recovering from setbacks or loss.

The main thing to realize is that happiness is always your *choice*. You have the right to be happy no matter what! And it's possible to get to this point. It's possible to have a mindset where you walk around with a sparkly, metaphorical cape that waves in the air behind you. To have a mindset where life happens, and you shrug, always looking to the bright side, asking,

> *"What great things may come of this?"*

There's always something. There are always other possibilities. Asking this question keeps your eyes on the prize.

Does that mean you're cold and indifferent when bad things happen to others? No. You're kind and sympathetic, but also a pillar of strength. You're spreading positive energy and love when they need it most. If something bad happens to someone you love, and you keep your spirits high, elevated, and happy, that helps you, them, and the world. There is no guilt about this. Ever. Feeling guilt won't help you or them.

Lastly... your permission slip also gives you all the right in the world to love yourself *as you are now*: your body now, your face today, your skin this minute, your living conditions now, your finances now, your career now... all of it.

There's *magic* in love, and when you love, you expand, and your energy attracts your dreams to you. And you have the right to all the happiness in the world, no matter what is happening. You have permission to shine like a *blazing star*, because that's what you are!

Your Turn to Play!

Create your own permission slip. Grab your notebook or a piece of paper, and write the following, filling in the blanks with whatever seems most important in your life right now:

I have the right to _____
I have the right to _____
I have the right to _____
I have the right to _____
I have the right to _____

Refer back to this list periodically over the next few days, and be mindful of the fact that you have permission to pursue whatever makes you happy, as you navigate your day-to-day life.

You're embracing your freedom.

Today's affirmation:

I have the right to be happy, no matter what.

CONCLUSION

Yay! Your tool kit for living a magical life just got more chunky and badass, with all kinds of great ways for navigating life and surfing its waves. The most important thing is to always be mindful that the words and thoughts you use—your self-talk—is *the* primary driver of living your happiest, most magical life. But for those times when you need a boost, or a strategy for dealing with a situation that arises, the techniques in this book can help.

Can I ask a favor of you, please? If you could leave a review for this book at Amazon, it makes a huge difference, and I'd *greatly* appreciate it! From my heart to yours, in gratitude.

It's only goodbye for now, but we can connect again in my other books listed in the back of this book. And I love hearing from readers, so shoot me an email and say hi!

Kristen@HappySexyMillionaire.me

Or connect with me on Instagram: @CoffeeSelfTalk

Oh! And check out our fabulous Coffee Self-Talk Facebook group:

facebook.com/groups/coffeeselftalk

It's filled with fun, loving, supporting people. The group blows my mind on a daily basis with the support and excitement that dances there.

See you inside!

FREE PDF

For a free, printable PDF with cut-out affirmations and fun reminders to hang on your refrigerator, email me at:

Kristen@HappySexyMillionaire.me

Please specify that you'd like the:

"Daily Reader #1 Fridge Stuff"

OTHER BOOKS BY KRISTEN HELMSTETTER

Coffee Self-Talk: 5 Minutes a Day to Start Living Your Magical Life

Coffee Self-Talk for Dudes: 5 Minutes a Day to Start Living Your Legendary Life

> *Coffee Self-Talk for Dudes* is 95% the same book as *Coffee Self-Talk*, but oriented toward men.

The Coffee Self-Talk Blank Journal (blank with lines)

Coffee Self-Talk for Teen Girls (coming 2021)

Pillow Self-Talk (coming 2021)

The Coffee Self-Talk Guided Journal (coming 2021)

ROMANCE NOVELS

Under the pen name Brisa Starr

Lockdown Love

His Secret

Save Me

Sweet as Pie

Fake It (Young Brothers Book I)

Count on Me (Young Brothers Book II)

Play Time (Young Brothers Book III)

Christmas Beauty (Young Brothers Book IV)

Made in the USA
Coppell, TX
09 September 2021

62083984R00095